PRAISE FOR ILL

"In *Illuminate*, Bethany Petty presents the wide-ranging spectrum of what is available in technology to schools and how it can be implemented. She generously shares her own experiences from the classroom in a conversational, friendly tone. If you're getting started with technology and want to know what's out there, this book is for you!"

—Matt Miller, blogger, speaker, and author of *Ditch That Textbook*

"*Illuminate* is exactly what every instructional technology coach needs on their first day on the job. It provides a complete blueprint for how to bring in EdTech into the classroom and provide quality coaching to teachers of all grade levels! The tips and tools in this book will allow every tech coach to focus on coaching instruction rather than the technology when working with their teachers."

—Jeffrey Bradbury, @TeacherCast, TeacherCast.net

"Bethany has created a practical technology integration guide that any teacher can follow, loaded with ideas to engage students and build critical thinking skills. This thoughtful book will help teachers build their digital toolbox and find the best tool for the job. And educators at every level will appreciate the handy tips and tricks!"

—Kasey Bell, teacher, speaker, and blogger at ShakeUpLearning.com

"Bethany has crafted a thoughtful text that speaks to the importance of bringing technology use into the classroom at deep, meaningful, sustainable levels. With practical tips and great resources, Bethany makes the fears around teacher use of technology dissolve. This book is an opportunity to learn, but it can also be a great catalyst for conversations throughout a school. Every reader will find something that they can use to engage and empower the students that they serve."

—Dr. Robert Dillon, author of *Leading Connected Classrooms* and *The Space: A Guide for Educators*

"With an infectious passion for the practical in helping engage students in their learning, and written in a lively style appealing to an educator looking for a friend in the classroom, in her book *Illuminate*, Bethany Petty, a 2017 EdTech Leadership Award honoree, provides an easy-to-apply rundown of what's relevant for any teacher looking for the right level of fun (a lot!) with some of the latest, greatest and most effective learning tools."

—Victor Rivero, editor-in-chief, *EdTech Digest*

"*Illuminate: Technology Enhanced Learning* by Bethany Petty offers some timely suggestions for educators to facilitate active learning opportunities for students. Educators reading this book will gain practical advice to help make learning stick through the purposeful integration of technology."

—Sarah Thomas, PhD, founder of EduMatch

ILLUMINATE

TECHNOLOGY ENHANCED LEARNING

BETHANY J. PETTY

Illuminate
© 2018 by Bethany Petty

This book is available at special discounts when purchased in quantity for use for premiums, promotions, fundraising, and educational use. For inquiries and details, contact us at books@daveburgessconsulting.com.

Published by Dave Burgess Consulting, Inc.
San Diego, CA
DaveBurgessConsulting.com

Editing and production by My Writers' Connection
Cover Design by Genesis Kohler
Author photo by PureSonic

Library of Congress Control Number: 2019950061
Paperback ISBN: 978-1-949595-83-3
eBook ISBN: 978-1-949595-84-0

For Hanna and Molly
You can do *anything* you set your minds to!

For Issac
Thank you for all your continuous love and
support of me and my crazy ambitions.

For Mom and Dad
Thank you for everything.

Contents

INTRODUCTION

Teachers, we live in a fantastic time in education. Our students have access to information like never before and have limitless potential to create amazing products. The availability of technology tools in the classroom can help our students be more engaged and connected than ever before!

If you don't consider yourself especially "tech-savvy," it may seem that using technology in the classroom comes easily for everyone except you. You may even have Chromebooks sitting around collecting dust because you aren't sure what to do with them or are afraid of messing them up. You aren't alone!

The sheer number of educational technology tools and websites can be overwhelming to teachers and students and can present a daunting challenge: How do I use all these technology tools in my classroom?

That isn't a bad question, but it can lead to an incorrect focus on using technology for the sake of using technology. If we are going to effectively incorporate tech devices and apps in our classrooms, our focus must be on using technology to enhance the learning environment. Notice the shift *away* from focusing on specific tools and finding ways just to use them and *toward* using technology—in any number of ways—to elevate lessons and help students learn.

Think of educational technology tools as a light switch in a dimly lit room. If you walk into a room without flipping on this light switch, you can probably still accomplish the task you set out to complete when you entered the room. Maybe you sit down to read a book. You stumble around to find a comfy chair, prop up your feet, open the book, and settle in to read your next favorite novel. Can you read the book? Sure, although you'll most likely strain your eyes trying to read the words. Could you enhance your reading experience by turning on the light? Absolutely! When used well, educational technology tools can enhance the learning experience for your students much like flipping on a light switch can improve your encounter with a great book.

You may say, skeptically, "Well, Bethany, humans have been reading words and interpreting images for much longer than the light bulb and electricity have existed, and teachers have taught without using educational technology tools." You're absolutely right! We didn't start using light bulbs to illuminate our homes because candles or lanterns stopped working. We use light bulbs and the electricity that powers them to enhance our lives in the same way teachers can use technology tools to enhance the learning environment for our students.

Notice, though, I haven't focused on the types of light bulbs, their wattage, lifespan, or energy efficiency rating in this description. Why? Simply because the light bulb is used to enhance our life, but it does not become the focus of life. I don't wake up in the morning excited about the wattage of the light bulbs in my house or worried about whether they are considered "green" or trendy. I flip on the light switch so I can find my way to the coffee maker.

As teachers, we do not (or at least we shouldn't) use technology tools because they are flashy or trendy, nor should these tools be the focus of our classroom. Our lessons do not focus on how to create screen-casts. Our units are not designed around using Edpuzzle or Flipgrid. We use technology tools to enhance learning for our students and to elevate their learning experience in our classroom. These tools are just that: tools. Our goal is to use them to encourage students to create, collaborate, communicate, think critically, reflect, and engage in content to apply their knowledge. After all, it's not about the technology; it's how you use it!

My goal with this book is to present some great educational technology tools that you can use in your classrooms within the context of how these tools can help students . . .

- **engage** in learning
- **explore** content

- **create** representations of their knowledge
- **communicate** their thoughts
- **think critically**
- **collaborate** with their peers both in the classroom and around the world
- **reflect** upon their knowledge and understanding

As well as how these tools can help you . . .
- **motivate** your students in a culture of instant gratification
- **connect** and learn from other teachers
- **assess** student knowledge
- **design** meaningful learning experiences for your students
- **reflect** upon your teaching

Each chapter includes strategies you can use alongside great technology tools to enhance the learning environment and increase student engagement in your classroom. Use the technology tool index at the back of the book as a quick reference guide to find and learn more about the tools mentioned in this book.

Are you ready? It's time to flip on the light switch and use technology to enhance learning!

CHAPTER 1
ENGAGE WITH TECHNOLOGY

How can you use technology to help your students become engaged in course content?

Our students live in an amazing, connected world that pulls them in many different directions. Imagine for a moment that you were a student in your classroom. How would your day unfold? What kinds of things might keep you from engaging in the lesson? I know every school is different, but if you were a student in my classroom, here's what your school life may look like:

You and every one of your classmates have a Chromebook provided by the school—which, by the way, is awesome. You sit at one of fifteen tables with one other student. I have arranged my tables into pods with a lone table in the front which serves many purposes, including an extra workspace for students and a place for me to perch while answering student questions. Nearly everyone in the classroom has a smartphone and earbuds and some people have tablets or iPads. Our school Wi-Fi restricts access to social media sites like Twitter or Facebook from their Chromebooks, but (fortunately) you can access YouTube. Personal smartphones are not connected to the school Wi-Fi, which means if your device allows for cellular data use, you can access social media that way. Of course, you also have books, folders, notebooks, and sketch-books at your workspace.

Do you have a picture in your head? Now, in addition to the things that occupy our students' physical space, sometimes they come to school carrying bulky baggage from their home life. Maybe they had an argument with their parents or siblings on the way to school that morning. Perhaps they're anxious about an after-school practice, game, or recital.

As you can see, our students sit in our classrooms with, believe it or not, other things on their minds than the lessons we share with them. *GASP* That's why we must be intentional about engaging our students—capturing and holding their attention and getting them to interact with our content.

How do we encourage our students to engage with our content? By meeting them where they are and pairing technology tools with sound educational strategies. Let's look at two ways to *engage* your students with technology and enhance their learning.

ENGAGE STUDENTS WITH VIDEO: The In-Class Flip

Most of our students probably have at least a basic understanding of the video tool that has taken the world by storm: YouTube. My daughters are 5 and 7 years old and love to watch makeup tutorials, toy unboxing videos, miniature-food creation shows, and the be-all-end-all of YouTube videos for kids, surprise eggs. If you are unfamiliar with videos about surprise eggs, imagine a video showing a variety of plastic Easter eggs (sometimes they're chocolate eggs) that are filled with a random variety of small toys, candy, or stickers. My young daughters are completely fascinated with what is in these eggs and will be glued to their iPads for far longer than I would like to admit, waiting to see what is unveiled.

My high school students are always plugged into YouTube, whether it be to listen to music while they work or to watch a funny or informational video. A few years ago, I decided to try to capitalize on this love of YouTube by flipping my classroom. The result exceeded my expectations, and I now use this strategy in my Government classes all the time.

In my American Government classroom, my students participate in a version of an in-class flip. My views on traditional homework have evolved during the years (I hate homework and don't assign it), so I decided to make better use of my instructional time to benefit my students. Instead of standing in front of the room for fifty minutes lecturing about the amazing and exciting concept that is the senatorial filibuster (I am a huge government geek), I decided to make instructional videos for my students to watch in class before starting on their activity for the day. Here's a rundown of how my flipped classroom works:

- Students view instructional videos created by me (3–5 minutes in length) via Edpuzzle for two to three days per week as a Bell Ringer/opening activity.
- Students interact with the video through embedded formative assessment.
- As they watch the video, students are taking notes on content on a Google Doc.
- As students finish their video assignment, they move to other coursework.

You may be asking yourself, *what does Bethany do while her students are working?* Since my students interact with the instructional video at the beginning of the class period, I use this time to take attendance (which I always forget to do), set up the classroom for the activity for the day, monitor student progress on Edpuzzle, and provide immediate feedback on their understanding of concepts I discuss in the video.

When all students have completed the instructional video, we play a quick game of Kahoot!, Quizizz, or Quizlet Live to ensure everyone is on the same page. The students who place in the top three as well as one student chosen at random earn Bonus XP. This Bonus XP, also called "experience points," is earned by students when they complete a variety of tasks, such as instructional videos, assignments, projects, etc. (We'll discuss more about gamification in Chapter 8.)

A flipped-classroom approach offers many benefits, but one of my favorite features is that students can interact with the video at their own pace. When I was a student, I was able to copy notes from the board and catch what the teacher was saying pretty quickly. I often ended up bored and frustrated that it took some of my classmates longer to catch up.

When I started teaching, I presented information the same way I had been taught. I strictly lectured. I felt frustrated when students asked me to go back to the previous slide, spell a specific word, or repeat myself. My flipped classroom eliminates these issues! My students view instructional videos individually, which lessens the influence of classroom distractions. Students can also pause and rewind my instruction as they need to. If some parts of the lesson just aren't "sticking," they can always access the video on YouTube to re-watch at any time. Another beneficial feature of the flipped classroom is that students have constant access to their teacher. Some of my students have referred to the flipped instructional model we use as having "my teacher in my pocket."

There are different schools of thought on basically every aspect of the flipped classroom, but much discussion surrounds the length of the video, teacher presence in the video, and whether the teacher has created the video or has selected a pre-existing video lesson for their students to view.

> Part of the beauty of the flipped classroom is that it provides great flexibility for teachers based on their students' needs.
>
> #ILLUMINATEED

My goal is to keep my instructional videos between three and five minutes in length. Some in the world of education say that videos should be less than one minute, others say eight minutes is the longest your video should ever be. Part of the beauty of the flipped classroom is that it provides great flexibility for teachers based on their students' needs.

I'm also a proponent of teacher presence in videos, which means I encourage teachers to make their own instructional videos. When I was experimenting with the flipped-classroom model, I decided to create an instructional video for my students on a day in which they would be having a substitute. (I was attending a technology conference.) I created my video using Explain Everything on my iPad and did not include an embedded video of myself talking in the video. My students freaked out! They said it seemed weird to hear my voice without seeing my face. They felt as if "the talking head of Mrs. Petty was teaching from somewhere," but they couldn't see me. I personally thought it would be strange to have my face in the video; however, my classroom exists to meet my students' needs rather than my own. After that, every video included an embedded video of me talking (and sometimes "rapping") about course concepts. While using pre-existing videos is just fine, I personally believe that creating instructional videos for my students is a powerful part of my flipped classroom. If I were to use a video created by a different teacher, I may lose legitimacy in the eyes of my students. They may feel as if the lesson I've prepared for them doesn't have great importance for me if I couldn't take the time to create the video myself. I never want students to feel slighted in my classroom.

Today, I use the Chrome extension Screencastify to create my instructional videos, which allows to me to easily record my screen, include an embedded video of me, and upload them to YouTube (more about Screencastify in Chapter 3).

Designing Video Lessons with Edpuzzle

Many great tools exist to help us create, edit, and assign video lessons to our students with embedded formative assessment questions. My absolute favorite tool to accomplish all these tasks is Edpuzzle (Edpuzzle.com). Full disclosure: Edpuzzle is a sponsor on my blog, but I would share this resource even if

Learn more about using
EDpuzzle in your classroom!
http://bit.ly/illuminate-edpuzzle
#illuminatedED

they weren't! I love that I can create individual classes and import my rosters from Google Classroom (saving a step for me *and* my students) and that I can view their progress on the videos while providing timely feedback on their responses. The Edpuzzle Chrome extension adds a button to any YouTube video that makes it easy to for teachers to edit the video, add it to their Edpuzzle library, and assign it to their students. Edpuzzle allows me to view student progress on videos across time *and* how many times they rewatch specific parts of the video. Having this information provides fantastic feedback for me on the instructional videos I create. I'm able to monitor student progress as they complete the lesson, observe how many times students view sections of the video, and provide immediate feedback to my students as they respond to embedded questions. Edpuzzle also offers a smartphone app for students (not yet available for the teacher dashboard, as of March 2018), which allows students to take their work anywhere. Even though I don't assign homework, the need sometimes arises for students to work on their videos outside of class because of absences. Likewise, through using HyperDocs in my classroom, I've noticed that some students prefer to work on their videos outside of the classroom to get ahead (more about designing lessons with HyperDocs in Chapters 7 and 9).

When designing video lessons, it's important to incorporate a variety of questions relating to the content that is the focus of the video. Equally important are those questions that require students to rely on prior knowledge as well as apply the content to multiple situations; for example, a video about the landmark Supreme Court case of *Marbury vs Madison* will include questions about the issues of the case and the role of the federal judiciary in applying the Constitution. A final question may ask students to determine whether the decision gave the Supreme Court too much power combined with asking them to support their opinion.

What are the benefits of utilizing video lessons as a means for delivering instruction?

- Students have constant access to content from their teacher.
- Students can revisit content information as much (or as little) as they need to.
- Teachers regain valuable instructional time and can design more meaningful activities to encourage application of knowledge.

The flipped classroom allows you to move from the "sage on the stage" to the "guide on the side" in the classroom by freeing you from being glued to the front of the room with your computer and projector. Rather than talking *at* students for the entire class period, a flipped-classroom approach gives you time and space to actually teach students and *interact* with them in groups or individualized experiences which can help students grasp concepts. And when students are allowed to work at a pace that fits their learning style, they begin to ask questions about the content as well as how they can apply what they're learning.

Using Nearpod to Engage Students in Content

As you continue reading this book, you'll no doubt notice I introduce quite a few tools as "one of my absolute favorites." I can't help it! I love using great tools to elevate my teaching and enhance the learning environment of my classroom, and one of my absolute favorite classroom tools is Nearpod (nearpod.com), an interactive lesson platform that allows you to create engaging presentations for your students.

I use Nearpod primarily in my dual-credit social studies classes. (Dual-credit classes are courses in which students earn high school and college credit simultaneously.) My goal is to create a blended learning environment in these courses in which I create and present interactive lectures (with Nearpod) for my students several days each week. Students use it to participate in online discussion boards along with reflective writing assignments and activities that require them to analyze primary and secondary sources. They also use it to create and share their understanding of those readings. Online discussion boards are a fantastic addition to my classes. One of the best characteristics of these activities is that they allow all students to be heard. Technology helps give all students a voice and a chance to interact in class discussions.

To use Nearpod, simply create an account. (Using the Google single sign-on is an option.) One of the great features of Nearpod is that you can upload presentations you have already created in Google Slides, Microsoft PowerPoint, or saved as a PDF. Once the file is uploaded, you can choose to display the presentation as a PDF file or as individual slides. I always choose individual slides so I can manage the slides more easily.

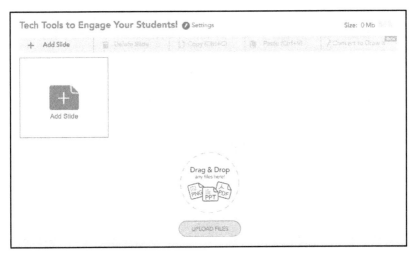

Here's where the magic happens. Nearpod allows you to embed formative assessment, websites, videos, brainstorming and collaborative activities, 3D elements, and—my favorite—virtual field trips into existing presentations. My students absolutely love touring places we learn about in class. I can't tell you how amazing it is to be able to take my students inside the barracks at Auschwitz, on the Arizona Memorial, and to modern-day Hiroshima and Nagasaki as we learn about World War II. They immediately become more engaged in the content as they experience it visually rather than through the words from a dusty textbook.

Students can take virtual field trips using Nearpod on any device, with or without a virtual reality viewer; in fact, I encourage my students to use multiple devices when we use Nearpod so they can view the presentation and take notes on their Chromebook, giving them a more immersive experience with the virtual field trips through their smartphone or tablet.

Students immediately become more engaged in the content as they experience it visually rather than through the words from a dusty textbook.

#ILLUMINATEED

I should mention that I do not require my students to take notes on their Chromebook or electronic device. Some of my students prefer to take notes on lecture and discussion by hand, and that is just fine with me. I always tell my classes that the notes they take in this classroom are to deepen their understanding of the content. If taking notes on a Chromebook helps them accomplish this task, then so be it. If they would rather take notes in a spiral-bound notebook, they can do it. After all, my classroom is about my students' learning, and I don't want to dictate to them how they should learn.

ENGAGE STUDENTS WITH QR CODES

If you walk into my classroom, you'll see a variety of strange-looking squares displayed on the walls, cabinets, shelves, desks, and even the presidential busts. You may see students standing in front of these images with a smartphone or a Chromebook. These students might be reading information, viewing a video, or responding to questions while standing in front of these images.

What exactly are these squares, and why does it seem like they are everywhere?

QR Codes, also called "quick response" codes, are images that, when scanned with a smartphone or other tech device, link to a specific website, text, image, or video.

QR Codes provide teachers with a great way to encourage their students to engage in the four Cs of twenty-first-century learning in different ways that feel far more exciting than simply typing in a URL while sitting at their desks.

QR Codes can be used in a variety of ways to make your classroom learning environment more exciting! Here are just a few examples:

Encourage Students to Explore

Placing QR Codes in various places around your classroom that link to additional course content can encourage students to move beyond what is expected of them in a lesson or assignment. If students finish an assignment or activity early, they can scan a QR Code that links to a game that relates to your content area. Maybe they can "get ahead" by watching a YouTube video that provides an overview of upcoming information.

Apply Knowledge with QR Code Scavenger Hunts

Creating scavenger hunts with QR Codes is a fun way for your students to apply what they've learned in your classroom. In

Learn more about using QR Codes in your classroom! http://bit.ly/illuminate-qr-codes #illuminatedED

my American Government class, my students frequently use QR Code scavenger hunts along with Google Forms to help apply knowledge of the three different branches of government. To be quite honest with you, I realized early on in my teaching career that not all my students would be as excited about the function and structure of the

American political system as I was. Not everyone "geeks out" about our intricate system of checks and balances, and that's just fine! QR Code scavenger hunts provide my students with real-world scenarios that require them to determine whether specific actions of members of the federal government are in accordance with the Constitution. Instead of me standing in front of my students and asking them about the applications of the Necessary and Proper Clause, they are up and moving around the room, communicating and collaborating with their group to check the actions of members of the Legislative Branch. It's beautiful to behold!

Direct Classmates to Additional Information

When my students create presentations or projects that will be printed and displayed in the classroom or the hallway, I always require them to include a QR Code that links to a resource about their topic. This resource could be a YouTube video, article, image, or a resource they have created themselves to help their peers understand a topic. During the 2016 Presidential Election, my American Political Systems students created profiles of the candidates that we displayed in the hallway outside my classroom. Each student included a QR Code that would direct someone to

Learn more about using QR Codes to direct students to additional information here!
http://bit.ly/illuminate-hashtags
#illuminatedED

additional information about the candidate. These QR Codes were linked to everything from the candidate's official website to videos of speeches to their social media accounts. As my students worked on this project, I encouraged them to think of the profile they were creating and the QR Code they included to be something of a public service to students (and adults) who were walking by their display. In other words, they needed to keep in mind the audience for whom they were creating these profiles. This helped provide my students with an authentic, real-world audience who would read and learn from their presentations.

Review Information

In my flipped classroom, I frequently use Tes Teach to help my students review content information. With Tes Teach, I can easily create a digital board of content to share with my students that provides them with all the unit information. From YouTube instructional videos to helpful diagrams we've created in class to review activities,

Learn more about using Blendspace by Tes Teach in your classroom!
http://bit.ly/illuminate-blendspace
#illuminatedED

games, and more, one QR code for a board gives my student access to a wealth of resources.

Share Important Course Information

The "Important Information" bulletin board in my classroom contains, obviously, information that students, administrators, and parents need to know about my class. QR codes on this bulletin board direct students and parents to my YouTube channel, class website, instructions on how to join the Remind messaging service, an "About the Teacher" video, course syllabus information, a video explaining how the flipped classroom works in our American Government course, and a document with my contact information. Why do I use QR codes to share this information? I like that anyone can quickly scan the code and access this information on a smartphone, tablet, or Chromebook.

How to Create QR Codes for Your Classroom
Chrome Extensions

If you're a Google Chrome user, Chrome extensions are an easy way to create QR codes. "My absolute favorite Chrome extension for QR Code creation is the Quick QR Code Generator extension, accessible through the Chrome web store.

To create QR Codes with the Quick QR Code Generator extension, access the Chrome Web Store and search for "Quick QR Code Generator," and choose the first option. A great tip for sifting through a multitude of search results in the Chrome Web Store is to look at the reviews that have been left by other users. Click the *+Add to Chrome* on the first extension that appears on the screen. When it's installed, you'll see a new icon for the extension in the toolbar at the top of your screen. Next, identify and go to an online resource you want to share with your students. This resource could be a YouTube video, Google Form, Padlet wall, Blendspace board, website, article—basically anything you can access from Google Chrome. Then click on the Quick QR Code Generator extension icon. You'll immediately see a window open that contains the QR Code to your resource. Beneath the image, you will see a blue QR! button. Below this image, you'll see the option to save the QR Code. You can also right-click on the QR Code to copy and paste or save it for later. This is a must-have extension!

Websites

Several websites make it easy and free to create QR Codes for your classroom. Among these are QR Code Monkey (qrcode-monkey.com) and QR Stuff (qrstuff.com). These websites give you the ability to create QR Codes from websites, images, and files and allow you to customize the appearance of your QR Code (shape, color, etc.).

Tes Teach (formerly known as Blendspace) is a great website that allows teachers to share collections of resources with their students through a single board. Using Tes Teach, I share course and/or unit information with my students using a QR Code I created through the site. I can print the QR Code and post it in my classroom, or I can copy and paste the QR Code on my digital materials! Sharing Tes Teach lessons and resources through QR Codes is a wonderful way for teachers to make information readily available for their students!

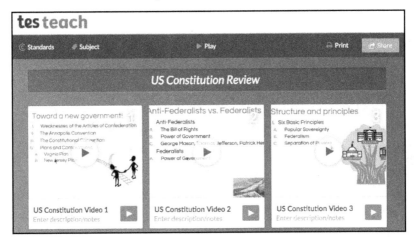

Google Sheets

Spreadsheets in any form, such as Microsoft Excel or Google Sheets, can be daunting and downright scary to use. This fear of using spread-sheets most likely comes from a lack of familiarity with them. I steered away from spreadsheets in the past because I didn't fully understand the possibilities they held for my classroom.

Google Sheets offers Add-ons, many of which are fantastic for the classroom. (Add-ons allow Google users to add more functionality to a host of Google tools.) QR Code Generator is an Add-on that allows you to easily create QR Code review activities directly from a Google Sheet. Since the activity is created in Google Drive, you can easily access and share the activity.

Create QR Codes with Google Sheets

1. Open a new Google Sheet.
2. In the Sheet, type information you wish to be accessible through the QR Code.
3. Access the Add-ons menu and select *Get add-ons . . .*
4. Type "QR Code Generator" in the search bar of the *Search add-ons* box.
5. Select the *+Free* button to add the QR Code Generator Add-on to your Add-on menu in Sheets.
6. Access the Add-ons menu again, choose *QR Code Generator,* and click *Open.*
7. Highlight the column that includes the information to become QR Codes.
8. Be sure *QR Code* is selected at the top of the dialogue box that appears.
9. Choose the desired QR Code size and select how the QR Codes should be saved. These options include a PNG file (mostly used for images) or as a Doc (which would be great for printing).
10. Select *Generate.*

After the QR Codes have been created by the Add-on, the QR Codes will be saved and downloaded in the file option you choose. You're then ready to print (or copy/paste) the QR Codes wherever you choose.

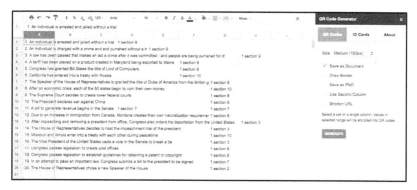

I use the QR Code Generator Add-on to make QR Codes for review activities (check the section on Engaging Students with QR Code), but the possibilities are endless with this great tool.

OTHER GREAT TOOLS TO PROMOTE ENGAGEMENT

On any given day in my classroom, the soft hum of "Aerosmith on the airwaves" or "Bach in the BACHground" plays in the background. (Yes, I am *that* teacher who makes and laughs at terrible puns.) My students enjoy the atmosphere of my classroom when they enter and hear music playing. By simply accessing my Pandora (Google Music, Spotify, etc.) account on my desktop, I can create a more inviting learning environment for my students.

While so many distractions constantly vie for our students' attention, we can encourage them to engage in our content by offering them a variety of options to take control of their learning. That's our goal: to encourage students to engage in content in a meaningful way that will make them want to dive in and explore further. And exploring with technology is where we're heading next.

Try This Tomorrow

Create a free account with Edpuzzle and begin searching for videos you could use in your classroom. Begin experimenting with the use of video lessons and reflect upon how you could use this strategy to enhance the learning environment in your classroom.

#ILLUMINATEED

Learn more about using technology tools to engage students in their learning at usingeducationaltechnology.com/engage.

Notes on Engaging with Tech

Chapter 2
EXPLORE WITH TECHNOLOGY

How do you encourage your students to explore, using technology?

Learning about the White House, the Great Pyramids, the Palace of Versailles, and marine life is great, but wouldn't it be even better to go to the White House? Unfortunately for most teachers, hopping on a plane with all their classes to jet to visit these places is just not in the cards or the budget. I often wish I had access to Ms. Frizzle's Magic School Bus, or Professor Dumbledore's ability to *apparate*, but alas, I do not! But I *do* have access to a *free* virtual tour of the White House—and so do you through a variety of great resources.

ENGAGE STUDENTS WITH VIRTUAL FIELD TRIPS

If you've never experienced a virtual field trip, you are missing out on some serious fun. A wealth of excellent apps exists today that makes it possible to take students on amazing trips around the world without ever leaving the classroom. I encourage you to leverage the power of virtual field trips and virtual reality in your classroom. It's fun to travel alongside students as they make discoveries about the world. Here are just a few ways to start exploring:

Virtual Field Trips with Google Earth

How would you rather learn about the world? Would you like to learn with worksheets and stagnant pictures? Or would you rather immerse yourself in a tour of distant and historic places?

I think we all know the answer, and Google Earth has the solution!

Google Earth provides anyone the opportunity to visit nearly any place in the world, virtually. Imagine teaching a lesson on the attacks on September 11, 2001 and being able to actually take your students to the memorials dedicated to those who lost their lives on that day. With Google Earth, you can do just that.

Today, anyone can easily access Google Earth from their Chromebook or desktop. This new version gives users the option to search Google Earth, use the "Voyager" option, go to a random location with the "Feeling Lucky" tool, bookmark specific places, and share links to locations through social media and Google Classroom. These are wonderful new additions that can help teachers and students explore the world without leaving the classroom.

When using Google Earth in my classroom, I typically use the search feature because I'm looking for a precise place to take my students; however, the Voyager option seems to be built for classrooms in that it includes a variety of modules geared toward specific aspects of education, including history, culture, nature, and sports. As a history teacher and geek, I love the "History" option, which allows my students to follow the journey of European explorers, immerse themselves in the beauty of the Taj Mahal, or explore the ruins at Machu Picchu without leaving their desk. Many of the resources included in Voyager can also be found at Google Arts and Culture (google.com/culturalinstitute/beta).

Explore with Virtual Reality

It's one thing to be able to show students pictures of far-off cities and amazing locations, but allowing them to experience these places through virtual reality or augmented reality can be quite powerful.

There is definitely no shortage of virtual reality apps and videos in the world of educational technology. But what is virtual reality?

According to the *English Oxford Living Dictionaries*, virtual reality is "the computer-generated simulation of a three-dimensional image or environment that can be interacted within a seemingly real or physical way by a person using special electronic equipment, such as a helmet with a screen inside or gloves fitted with sensors." Virtual reality apps and videos use stereoscopic images that, together with a VR viewing device (headset, Google Cardboard, etc.) provide users with an immersive experience, giving them the feeling of actually being in a specific location.

Virtual Reality with YouTube

When you're ready to dive into the world of virtual reality, start with YouTube's official virtual reality channel. To get started, simply access the YouTube app on your smartphone and search for "Virtual Reality." You'll be able to access the Virtual Reality channel and view hundreds of great videos ranging from the 2017 Solar Eclipse to a hang glider over the ocean, and even a guided tour of Rome. Grab your VR viewer, select the virtual reality option on the YouTube video (this only works on virtual reality videos), slide your phone into your viewer, and get ready for an awesome experience!

Access YouTube's official Virtual Reality channel! http://bit.ly/illuminate-vr #illuminateED

These videos can be viewed without a virtual reality viewer and are still awesome, even on a desktop computer. Using tools like Google Expeditions and Google Cardboard, you can use virtual reality to take students on guided tours around the world without leaving their classroom.

Instructional technology tools provide teachers with endless possibilities for designing engaging activities for students. We are living in a world that is flooded with technology. As teachers, we can harness the power of technology tools to make learning exciting for our students. By flipping on the educational technology light switch, you can enhance your students' learning experience. When we can create activities that use technology tools that encourage them to explore new places, ideas, or concepts, they become more connected and involved in their learning experience.

Try This Tomorrow

Take your students to far-off places through Google Earth for Chrome. When you find a location, use the "Share to Classroom" extension to push the destination to your students' devices. How did this enhance the learning environment in your classroom? Share your experiences on Twitter!

#ILLUMINATEED

Learn more about encouraging your students to explore with technology at usingeducationaltechnology.com/explore.

Notes

English Oxford Living Dictionaries, 2017, s.v. "Virtual reality," en.oxforddictionaries.com/definition/virtual_realty.

Dictionaries, 2017, en.oxforddictionaries.com/definition/virtual_reality.

Notes on Exploring with Tech

Chapter 3
Create with Technology

 Encouraging students to create representations of their knowledge can help them own their learning. How do your students "create" in your classroom?

When I was in school, I loved creating poster projects and brochures. I loved the creative aspect of the project: the markers, the glue, the construction paper. All the pretty features of my posters and brochures made my overachieving heart smile. I also loved displaying the research I had gathered in an eye-catching product.

Is it wrong to love to create posters and brochures? Absolutely not! But given the remarkable technology our students can access in our classrooms today, why would we limit them to creating posters and brochures? Why not encourage our students to create products that convey what they've learned in a way that can be instantly published and shared?

Imagine how knowing your work could be seen by anyone in the world, rather than "just" your teacher, will impact the product you create. Over the past few years, I've emphasized with my students the idea that they should create projects and other work in class as if they were going to present their work to a future employer as an example of their skills. I will never forget the expressions on the faces of my students the first time I introduced this idea to them. I could nearly see the light bulbs blazing in their minds as they began to rethink the work they shared with me. If I'm expecting their work to be presented at a high level, shouldn't I elevate the projects and classwork above posters, brochures, and worksheets?

As you'll notice in Chapter 8, one of the goals I've set for myself as a teacher is to provide students with more choice. As a student,

I loved creating poster projects. I loved writing essays. Research papers that required me to analyze primary and secondary sources to answer a historical question made me *happy*. I've realized, however, that all students do not share my love for traditional assignments and projects. And still, teachers—myself included—tend to cling to teaching the way we were taught. The problem is that in doing so, we limit our students. The technology we and our students have access to in our classrooms today has the potential to create a learning environment

And still, teachers—myself included—tend to cling to teaching the way we were taught.

#ILLUMINATEED

that is much different than the classrooms of our school days. Students can use technology to create amazing representations of their knowledge. In this chapter we will explore a variety of creation tools and ideas that you can use to enhance the learning, retention, and reflection of your students.

CREATING SCREENCASTS TO DEMONSTRATE LEARNING

I love when my students create screencasts for my class because I can see their thinking in real time. Screencasting allows students to communicate information that they would typically present in front of the class using any web tool, such as Slides or a Google Site. So why would I have my students create a screencast instead of a traditional presentation? Creating screencasts allows them to think through their content and the way they want to deliver their presentation. This is also helpful for students who feel paralyzed at the thought of talking in front of a classroom full of their peers.

As my students prepare to present for the first time in my classroom, I share procedures for being a presenter and for being an audience member. I remind my students that it's not polite to snicker at or make fun of a classmate who is struggling with their presentation. We use "snaps" at the end of presentations instead of clapping to prevent "the slow clap" from taking over the classroom.

When I assign a presentation, I share with my students that maybe, *just maybe*, giving presentations in front of a room full of classmates is not everyone's cup of tea (or coffee, in my case). Some of their peers would probably much rather be just about anywhere other than presenting their work to a room full of people. I tell them that their dear coffee-infused teacher, who often dances around the classroom and raps about course concepts, was once *terrified* to speak in front of her class. Their response is priceless! "*You* were afraid to speak in front of people? You do that for a living!"

Yes, at one point in our lives, each of us has had to make a presentation or give a speech that we were not entirely excited to share. Yes, when our students leave our classrooms they will most likely be required to give presentations or speeches and stand in front of hosts of people to share some sort of information; however, if I can use technology tools to offer my students more choice in creating and delivering projects, especially if those tools ease their anxiety and allow them to create a better product, why would I not jump on that opportunity? Screencasting and the ability to use technology to communicate ideas and opinions is a skill that is becoming increasingly relevant in today's society.

Screencasts are a great way for students to show their understanding of a concept. Screencasts are also an excellent way for you, as the teacher, to create instruction modules. And once the screencast is created, you or your students can share them through YouTube, Drive, or other digital avenues. For students, sharing out their work to a real-world audience encourages them to produce high-quality work.

I hope the lightbulbs are starting to come on in your own mind as you consider how to use screencasting. Here are a few suggestions for what you can create:

- instructional videos for content
- procedural videos for course information
- personalized substitute lessons for your students
- detailed instructions for projects, activities, etc.

And if you're wondering how students can use screencasts in the classroom, consider the following ways they could use these videos to demonstrate mastery:

- videos of Google Slides presentations
- article reviews
- demonstrations
- book discussions

Get Started with Screencasting

Of the many screencasting tools available today, my favorite is Screencastify, a Chrome extension that allows me to create a video from a website, my desktop, or my laptop camera. Screencastify is a free tool that offers a premium paid version. (The premium version offers additional editing and downloading options.) Screencastify allows me and my students to easily create screencasts and share these videos through Google Drive or YouTube.

To get started with Screencastify, access the Chrome web store and search for "Screencastify" in the extensions. The Screencastify icon will be added to your Chrome extensions bar. When you access Screencastify, you will be prompted to choose a destination for your videos: either the device you are using or Google Drive. As a huge Google Drive fan, I direct my videos to be stored in my Google Drive, which allows me to access the videos I create even if I'm not using my personal computer.

Screencastify offers three recording options if your device has a webcam: "tab," "desktop," and "cam." I most often use the "tab" recording option when creating instructional videos for my students because I create these screencasts from a Google Slides presentation. When recording your videos, pay close attention to the specific options in the Screencastify extension; for example, make sure your microphone is selected before you begin recording! If you want to include a video of yourself as you create the screencast, be sure you have selected the appropriate box.

When you've completed your screencast, you will be able to save the video to your Google Drive or share the video on YouTube. When I create instructional videos for my students, they are shared with the world on my YouTube channel; however, when my students create screencasts for projects in my class, I allow my students to share a YouTube or Google Drive link to their video.

CREATING BOOKSNAPS TO DEMONSTRATE LEARNING

Do you teach with novels, articles, or any text? Do you require your students to take notes on their reading? Do your students use Snapchat? Do they have access to a smartphone/tablet camera?

If you answered yes to any of these questions, then BookSnaps are a perfect addition to your classroom. BookSnaps encourage students to interact with the text they're reading, share their thoughts, and use a medium with which they are probably quite comfortable.

The brain behind BookSnaps is the fabulous Tara Martin (@TaraMartinEDU), and I highly encourage you to check out the resources on her website and follow her on Twitter. The premise of a BookSnap is to actively read, snap a picture of text that you find important, annotate the text, and then share it through social media.

As I was reading *Ditch That Textbook* by Matt Miller, I created BookSnaps to reflect upon my own understanding and share my thoughts with readers on my blog. To create these BookSnaps, I simply took a picture of an important text using my iPhone, then annotated it with my Snapchat app. Here are a few examples:

If your students use Snapchat, they can snap their picture through the app or upload it from their photo library. Through Snapchat, students can then annotate the text they've "snapped," add drawings or Bitmoji images to the text, and share them via Snapchat. If your students are not Snapchat users, never fear! Google Drawings are another great way to create visual representations of understanding. If you would like your students to submit their BookSnaps, you can easily create a Dropbox for images via Google Classroom or Google Forms.

Google Forms and Google Classroom Dropbox

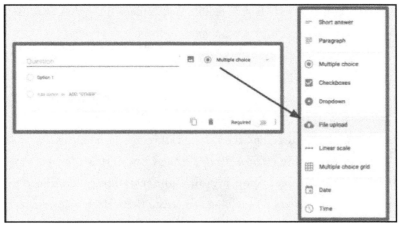

Create a File Upload Dropbox in Google Forms

1. Create a Google Form.
2. Include identifying questions such as "name," "class period," etc.
3. Create a new question and select "File Upload" instead of the default "Multiple Choice."
4. Select "Continue" if you are prompted by a message stating users will need to sign in to their Google account to upload files.
5. Choose to allow specific file types or allow any file uploads.
6. Choose maximum files and file sizes.
7. Be sure to send your responses to a Spreadsheet!
8. That's it!

Google Classroom Dropbox

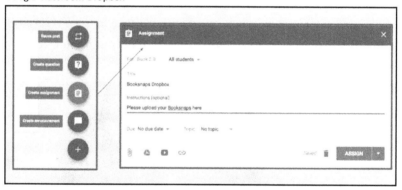

How to Create a File Upload Dropbox in Google Classroom

1. Create an assignment in Classroom.
2. Title your assignment and include directions for your students to follow when uploading their BookSnaps.
3. Select the classes and/or students to assign.
4. Students can choose to upload their BookSnaps from their device or from their Drive.
5. Monitor student progress through Classroom.
6. That's it!

BookSnaps are a fantastic way for students to create a product to display their understanding of a concept. They can also share these

BookSnaps through social media with their friends and with the world. This possibility places a whole new emphasis on creating a quality product.

CREATING MEMES TO DEMONSTRATE LEARNING

We live in a world of memes. Some of them are fabulous, while other memes are less than tactful. Memes can be a powerful way for students to convey their understanding of a topic or concept and can be used in a variety of interesting ways in the classroom. In short, memes are awesome!

A few years ago, I decided to make my back-to-school presentation more exciting and engaging for my students. Instead of droning on about procedures and expectations for my students through a mind-numbingly boring presentation, I spiced up my information with memes.

I used memes to convey important classroom information, procedures, and expectations to my students, and guess what? My students were engaged in what I was communicating. Even as they laughed at the meme about our classroom expectation concerning respect, I know it got the point across in a memorable way.

Your students can also create memes to show their understanding of a topic. As with other creation tools, when our students take something they have learned in class and create a fun product with that knowledge, they are likely to develop thorough understanding of that concept.

As a bonus mission in my American government class at the end of the year, my students create memes to explain a course concept or to provide advice for future students. The memes my students create about my class are awesome and sometimes quite eye-opening.

How to Create Memes with IMG Flip

Students can create memes using a variety of websites; my favorite is IMG Flip (imgflip.com).

To get started, simply access IMG Flip, select "Create," and choose "Caption a Meme or Image." One of the many great aspects of IMG Flip is that it offers a library of popular memes and images that are available for you and your students to caption. By using these popular memes and images to create information, teachers are speaking their students' language and meeting them where they are.

CREATING INTERACTIVE TIMELINES AND PRESENTATIONS

While creating poster projects and timelines may seem like an "old school" activity, they can easily be "techified" with a few great tools. These activities can encourage students to demonstrate their under-standing of content in creative, fun ways!

Creating Interactive Timelines with Sutori

As a high school social studies teacher, thinking about timelines makes my history-loving heart pitter patter! But the days of requiring my students to create a timeline using multiple pieces of poster board while using dated textbooks and encyclopedias are over. Today my students use digital timelines to visualize historical information. Sutori, formerly known as HSTRY, is an online interactive timeline creator that allows students to collaborate with each other to create informative and attention-grabbing presentations.

Teachers can create a free account using their Google single sign-on login information. This option means that our students don't have to remember (or, in my case, forget) yet another username and password. Teachers can then create groups in Sutori and invite students to join through a code, similar to Google Classroom or learning management systems. When students join, they will be able to create their interactive timeline project and can include a variety of informative sections:

- Text
- Image
- Video
- Audio
- "Did You Know?"
- Multiple Choice
- Matching Quiz
- Forum
- Heading

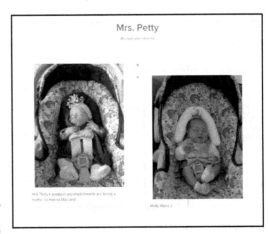

Students can easily add these sections in any order and can quickly drag the sections to reorder them.

Students can also collaborate with their classmates through Sutori by inviting them through email. Teachers are also able to view student work through Sutori. It's great!

Sutori also offers teachers the ability to share timelines that have been created by the teacher, student, or another Sutori user through URL, social media, email, embed code, or Google Classroom! Teachers can also share presentations they have made or found through Sutori with groups they have created.

Creating Interactive Presentations with Nearpod

Many teachers may think of Nearpod as a presentation tool to deliver engaging and interactive lessons created only by teachers. Nearpod, however, can also be used by our students to create fantastic presentations for their peers.

In my social studies classes, I use Nearpod to deliver lecture presentations, and my students use this tool to share their learning. During one of the summer session I teach, my students had just completed a timeline project about Roman emperors and their impact on the Roman world and were about to present their work. It just so happened that a new roof was being put on our building right when it was time for the presentations. I'm sure you have taught during many disruptions during your teaching career that are far worse than the constant hammering and drilling of roof replacement. I, however, didn't want my students to endure this disruption during their presentations.

I was faced with a conundrum: Do I forgo the presentations because of the roof repair sounds? Do I push the presentation off to another day? No! I wasn't about to allow our instructional activities to be derailed by roof repair.

My students and I moved our class to a different location for the day and proceeded with presentations. Because my students were going to be presenting their Sutori timelines, many of them were concerned about not having a projector/whiteboard in our new location. This is one of my favorite features of Nearpod: Teachers and students can take learning anywhere with no projector needed.

I collected the URLs from each student's Sutori presentation, created a Nearpod lesson, and shared the Nearpod code with my students. They were all able to view the collection of timelines on their own devices. Nearpod makes it easy for students to access presentations and follow along with the ones created by their classmates, and—probably most importantly for our students—know when they will present their own timelines because they can see the order of their presentations.

My students have also used Nearpod to present individual presentations they have created with Google Slides and in so doing have surprised me with the quality of their work. Combining Nearpod and Google Slides empowers users to embed videos, websites, images, and activities into presentations.

Whether you're in your classroom, are displaced because of building repairs, or are working in a virtual setting, Nearpod presentations make it easy for everyone to follow along.

Creating Graphics and Images for Presentations

Many great tools are available for teachers and students who wish to create images and graphics for their presentations. Canva, Adobe Spark (spark.adobe.com), and Google Drawings all make it easy to create and share graphics.

Both Adobe Spark and Canva provide premade templates that are sized perfectly for a variety of products, including social media images (Instagram, Twitter, Facebook, YouTube), marketing materials, posters, and more. Anyone can create a free account with Canva and Adobe Spark and can get started creating beautiful and informative graphics. Canva is frequently chosen in my classroom by my students for demonstrating their understanding of content.

CREATING VIRTUAL REALITY

It doesn't matter if you are a student or a teacher, virtual reality is awesome. It's fun to put on a VR headset and be transported to far-off places. As fun as that is, imagine the sense of empowerment your students will feel when you flip the light switch of educational technology and encourage them to *create* their own VR content!

My students really enjoy participating in global collaborations projects with classes from other parts of the world. We use great tools like Padlet and Google Hangouts to introduce and discuss our culture with students in other countries. During a recent collaboration activity, my students expressed an interest in sharing an image or video of our classroom with our overseas counterparts; instead, I offered to help them create virtual reality images of our classroom and other areas in our school. Watching a video of or viewing an image of a specific place is great, but immersing yourself in a new place using a virtual reality headset provides a whole different experience. The experience (both creating and watching VR material) takes learning to a new level and encourages students to use technology to connect with others around the world in a positive way.

Simple Steps to Using Google Street View to Create VR Content

Using free tools like Google Street View, students and teachers can create virtual reality trips to share with the world. To get started, simply download the Google Street View app with your iOS or Android device. Then open the app and select the camera icon in the bottom right of the screen. You'll be able to "link to external 360 camera,"

Learn more about using Google Street View to create VR images. http://bit.ly/illuminate-streetview #illuminateED "import 360 photos," or select "camera." If you choose "camera," you'll likely be prompted to grant the app access to your camera and photos. You're then ready to create VR content.

When you begin creating VR content with your smartphone, you'll start by capturing an image. As the image registers, you'll notice yellow dots appear on your smartphone. To include all angles in your VR content, simply move your smartphone to capture the small yellow circles that appear on your screen. When you're finished with your content, you'll click the checkmark on your screen and choose whether to publish your content publicly or save the content privately.

Found at the top of Bloom's Taxonomy, "creating" representations that demonstrate concept understanding is a vital skill that students must exercise as citizens of the twenty-first century. The International Society for Technology in Education (ISTE) identified the ability to effectively communicate thoughts and ideas as an essential skill and standard for students in the twenty-first century. When students create projects that demonstrate their understanding of course concepts, they take ownership in that project and pride in their learning. Encouraging students to create in your classroom can increase student engagement and develop an environment that invites students to take an active role in their learning.

Try This Tomorrow

Access a meme creator like IMG Flip and create a meme to describe a course procedure or concept. You will definitely grab your students' attention! Share your experience on Twitter!

#ILLUMINATEED

Learn more about encouraging your students to create with technology at usingeducationaltechnology.com/create.

Notes on Students Creating with Tech

Chapter 4
COMMUNICATE WITH TECHNOLOGY

How can we use instructional technology to encourage students to communicate in the classroom?

How can effective use of instructional technology include all students in classroom discussions and activities?

Communication is essential for success both in our classrooms and out in the "real world." Our students are entering a society vastly different from fifty, twenty-five, even ten years ago, and being able to effectively communicate their thoughts, opinions, and ideas is vital.

When I started my first year as a teacher in August of 2008, I was fresh out of college and, to be quite honest, scared to death to be in my own classroom. I was twenty-two years old teaching sophomores and juniors in high school. My undergraduate education had been great, but I don't think anything can *really* prepare a person to teach in a classroom of their very own. Added to the typical first-time jitters was the fact that my Dad underwent brain surgery on my very first day of class. (Don't worry, he's fine.) All the engaging, forward-thinking instructional strategies I had learned in college went out the window, and I began teaching like I had been taught in high school. I displayed a Microsoft PowerPoint presentation on the whiteboard, I created (and photocopied) worksheets to distribute to my students, had my students write "judicial opinions" by hand, and only required them to communicate their understanding on a unit assessment.

I expected my students to learn in the "sit and get" method, and any disruption seemed to be, in my first-year teacher eyes, a reflection of my classroom management style.

Yikes!

I have grown exponentially since my first year of teaching. *Thank goodness.* In my classroom today, I encourage my students to communicate their understanding of concepts, thoughts, and ideas as much as possible, using fantastic educational technology tools. After all, our students live in the twenty-first century. When they leave our classrooms, they must be

Why would I illuminate my classroom with a candle when I can use a light bulb? Why should we cling to and demand analog products in a digital world?

#ILLUMINATEED

ready to take on the twenty-first-century world. Why would I illuminate my classroom with a candle when I can use a light bulb? Why should we cling to and demand analog products in a digital world?

The short answer is, we shouldn't. In this chapter, we'll explore a variety of instructional strategies and technology tools to enhance student learning and elevate our teaching, specifically in respect to the ways we communicate and ask our students to share their learning.

COMMUNICATE THROUGH BLOGGING WITH GOOGLE SITES AND GOOGLE CLASSROOM

Most of the examples I use in this book come from my classroom experience, but this one comes from home. I have two daughters, ages four and six as of this writing, and they are beautiful and wonderful and lovely. As a doting mother, the list of fabulous adjectives I could use to describe my daughters is unending. Back to the story! My oldest, Hanna, will enter first grade in the fall. She is an excellent reader; however, for the longest time, she refused to read books. She would read anything and everything she encountered while we were out and about but had no desire to read books. It made my reading-loving heart hurt. One day during the summer, as we were eating lunch, I told her we were going to go to the library to get some new books to read. Her response was the typical, "Mom! I don't want to!" Right then and there, I decided I *had* to find some way to make reading a fun and exciting experience for her. Yes, I had already encouraged her to pick her own books and find genres that she may like, and yes, I had eBooks loaded on her iPad. I thought I had tried it all. Then that afternoon, I asked her if she wanted to review the books she picked out at the library on a blog, like Mommy. Her beautiful blue eyes lit up and she squealed, "Yes!" She then asked if she could read the books and put them on YouTube. Like many kids her age, Hanna loves to watch YouTube tutorials, so reading a book on YouTube was the perfect motivation for her to read. (You can bet I said yes to her request!)

As soon as we came home from the library, I created a blog for her using Google Sites. There are many great blogging platforms, including Blogger, which is part of Google accounts, Wordpress (which I use for my blog), Weebly, Edublogs; the list goes on and on. I chose to create Hanna's book blog using Google Sites because I knew it was easy to maintain and share. Part of the appeal of blogging to Hanna was that she would be able to share her thoughts on the books she reads with people she knows. She has currently challenged herself to read fifteen million books and blog about each of them. Blogging about what she reads has helped her become excited about reading and has led to an increased drive to read more!

In addition to teaching high school social studies, I am also an adjunct instructor for our local community college, where I teach Educational Technology in an online learning environment. One of my goals through this course is to offer preservice teachers the ability to construct their own knowledge and understanding of the possibilities that educational technology tools have in the classroom. Since Google Classroom is a staple in classrooms around the world, I decided to use this tool as a blogging platform for my adult students. I want them to see that, although Google Classroom is often used as a document-management system, it can be so much more.

To set up the blog post for this class, I created an assignment using the "question" option on Google Classroom. This allows my students to reply with their initial post, and then respond to their other classmates' posts within the assignment on Google Classroom. This also makes providing feedback a breeze. In my high school social studies classes, instead of creating a blog assignment for each class, I create a separate Google Classroom section for blog posts. This is used as an extension activity in which my students can earn Bonus XP (more about my motivational strategies in Chapter 8).

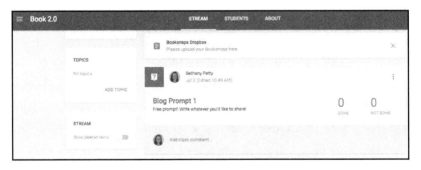

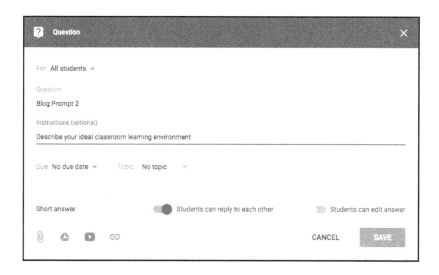

COMMUNICATE WITH FLIPGRID

Flipgrid is a fantastic tool on the EdTech scene that allows students to communicate their ideas and opinions in a brief video. Teachers can create a "grid" for their classes and then create topics within those grids to which students respond. Each grid houses topics that are created for and assigned to classes. Grids and topics can be shared via Google Classroom, URLs, embed code on a blog, QR Codes, or via Facebook or Twitter. Students respond to the topic with a brief video between thirty seconds and three minutes. Teachers can set a variety of requirements for their grids, such as requiring students to enter a password to access the grid. Teachers can also provide their students with timely feedback on their grids by requiring students to include their email addresses in the submission process. Using Flipgrid, students access a grid created by their teacher. The teacher shares a topic with the students, and the students respond to the topic by creating a video. Flipgrid uses a quick, four-step process for video creation and can be shared publicly or locked down for students and the teacher only. One of the many features of Flipgrid is that students can reply to their classmates' posts (if the teacher makes this option available). Commenting on and "liking" students' posts can be a powerful tool. When students know their work will be viewed not only by their teacher but also by their peers, it can encourage them to put more thought and effort into the product they are creating. Technology use can encourage all students to be part of the conversation.

Get Started with Flipgrid

To get started with Flipgrid, sign up for an account at flipgrid.com.

Technology use can encourage all students to be part of the conversation.
#ILLUMINATEED

Below are a few of the endless ways you can use Flipgrid to encourage students to communicate their thoughts and ideas:

Weekly Review

Students, especially in the upper levels, can review a current events article or news story, sharing multiple perspectives on the event with their peers. Students can share these videos through a school website or display them as QR Codes in various places around the school as a project to keep their peers informed of what is happening in the world around them.

Lifestyles of the Rich and Famous(ish)

Students in social studies classes can choose a historical figure who may not receive much attention in traditional narratives and describe, in a brief video, how that person impacted history. Ask them to try to persuade their peers, teacher, or an administrator to learn more about the individual's contributions.

Favorite Facts about Me

Students, especially in the elementary levels, can use Flipgrid to create an "About Me" report to share with their peers. This could be created at an open house event or beginning of the school year to share information with their classmates and their teacher!

What I've Learned So Far

Students can create brief videos of their favorite activities, projects, or concepts they've learned to share with their parents, teachers, and other school leaders for parent-teacher conferences or other meetings.

My Goals for Me

Students can set specific academic or personal goals that they can revisit throughout the year with their teacher, administrators, peers, and parents.

COMMUNICATE WITH GOOGLE HANGOUTS

Google Hangouts video calls can help take learning to a new level by encouraging communication with experts, authors, and even other classrooms beyond the walls of your school. While reading a novel about the Civil Rights Movement, for example, students can participate in a Google Hangout with the author of the book or with someone who participated in marches or other activities that took place during the setting of the book. While discussing the structure and function of the legislative branch in a government class, students can participate in a Google Hangout with their elected representative. Learning about a topic from an expert in the field helps make content real for students. When students see course content in action, they become more engaged and excited to learn about it.

A few years ago, I was looking for a way to enhance our unit on the legislative branch. This unit begins each year right after the Christmas break and, to be honest, not *everyone* is excited to be back in school. With that in mind, I wanted to find a way to really hook my students into learning in the new semester, so I decided to contact

 When students see course content in action, they become more engaged and excited to learn about it.

#ILLUMINATEED

our elected representative in the hopes of inviting him to speak to my class. I knew getting him to visit our school was a longshot because, just like everyone else, our legislators are busy people, and they often spend long periods of time in Washington DC instead of in their home district or state. That said, I thought that *anything* that could engage my students in the material was worth the effort. I called the local office, introduced myself, and asked if there was any way our congressman would be able to speak to my students. I offered the possibility of a Google Hangout video call if he wasn't able to speak to us in person.

The longshot paid off! Our congressman was very interested in speaking to my classes through a video call, and his staff in our local district and Washington DC were excited to make it work. While our congressman was in his office in our nation's capital, my students and I were able to ask questions, learn about his responsibilities, and see his office. At my students' request (they were begging), I asked a sitting United States congressman to take a selfie with us through a video call. Fortunately, he happily obliged. Using Google Hangouts allowed my students to connect and communicate with an expert in the field they were studying. Yet another example of how flipping the light switch of technology tools was able to enhance the learning experience for my students. Talk about engagement!

COMMUNICATE WITH PADLET

Padlet has so many classroom uses, and you'll notice that it's mentioned quite a bit in this book. Padlet is an online tool that lets teachers create "padlets" where students can collaborate, share ideas, present mini research projects, and so much more.

One of my favorite ways to use Padlet in my high school social studies classroom is to encourage students to be more engaged in historical or course-related films. Instead of completing a viewing guide while they watch videos, my students use Padlet to reflect upon the film.

In my American government classes, my students watch the movie *Lincoln*. This movie is absolutely phenomenal. It's wonderful. It's brilliant. But it can become dry for high school students because it's not an action movie. To keep students engaged both in the film and the course content that is reflected in the film (we watch historical movies to visualize what we're learning), students interact on a Padlet wall while we watch. These movie Padlet walls replace the old, dry, boring viewing guides that so often accompanied movie days in the classroom. The Padlet walls my students participate in while viewing films encourage them to compare historical events or government processes as they are portrayed in movies to "how it actually happened," while asking questions about specific characters' motives, actions, and accomplishments throughout the film. Padlet provides a great way for students to communicate through a backchannel while viewing course-related content.

Get Started with Padlet

To get started with Padlet, create an account at padlet.com. Padlet has a variety of account options from which to choose. The free version currently (as of April 2018) allows users to create three padlets. When users reach their padlet quota, they can simply delete previously used padlets.

Create a Padlet Wall

1. Access your Padlet account.
2. Select +*NEW* in the top right corner.
3. Choose your layout or theme.
4. Rename your Padlet wall and edit the site description (not required, but helpful for students).
5. Choose a wallpaper (background) for your Padlet wall, or upload or search for an image specific to your site's purpose.
6. Choose to turn on attribution and commenting (both are fantastic options that encourage collaboration) as well as the profanity filter, which replaces inappropriate words with an emoji.
7. Tag the Padlet wall if you'd like. (This makes searching for your Padlet in your account easier.)
8. Choose a customized URL for your Padlet (one of my favorite features because it allows me to more easily share the wall).
9. Select the *SHARE* option on the top of the Padlet.
10. When you share your Padlet wall, students will be able to write on it and view others' posts. You can choose to moderate posts.

Learn more about using the Share to Classroom extension in your classroom!
http://bit.ly/illuminate-share
#illuminateED

When your Padlet wall is complete, you'll be able to share it with your students by link, QR Code, Google Classroom, or with the Share to Classroom extension.

Padlet walls provide students and teachers with a great opportunity to communicate thoughts, opinions, ideas, research, and other important information in a collaborative environment.

There are endless possibilities for using Padlet in the classroom, including:

- Sharing course resources (class website, syllabus, field trip information, course procedures, etc.)
- Introducing students and/or teacher
- Sharing/uploading/capturing videos or images
- Posting review questions
- Classroom backchannel

COMMUNICATE WITH ANSWER GARDEN

Answer Garden (answergarden.ch) is a simple, effective tool that allows you to quickly gather and display information from students in a word cloud. Phrases or words that are submitted to word cloud generators like Answer Garden are displayed larger based on how many students share a specific response. This allows you to actually view student understanding.

You can choose to require a password for Answer Garden contributors and moderate student responses before they appear on the screen. You also have the option to allow individual students to submit as many responses as they would like while only allowing an answer to appear once, or you can choose to allow students to brainstorm, which permits students to submit as many answers and as many copies of each answer as they would like. You can also choose the length of student responses: twenty or forty characters. I love this feature because it requires students to really think about the response they are submitting and to be concise with their submission.

Learn more about using Answer Garden to collect evidence of student learning! http://bit.ly/illuminate-answer-garden #illuminateED

The ability to communicate effectively through the medium of technology is a vitally important skill for our students to master. Use the ideas and tools identified throughout this chapter to design lessons and activities that encourage your students to effectively communicate their ideas.

Try This Tomorrow

Poll your students about whom they would like to contact to learn more about a topic they're studying. Maybe a meteorologist, an author, an elected representative, a doctor, lawyer, or another professional. Reach out to these individuals through email and ask if they would be interested in participating in a Google Hangout with your class. It doesn't hurt to ask! Share your experiences with others on Twitter!

#ILLUMINATEED

Learn more about how your students can communicate with technology at usingeducationaltechnology.com/communicate.

Notes on Communicating with Tech

Chapter 5
USE TECHNOLOGY TO ENCOURAGE COLLABORATION AND CRITICAL THINKING

How can we create a learning environment that promotes collaboration and critical thinking? How can technology tools help us do so?

Take a trip in a time machine with me. What did your high school classroom look like? Your middle school classroom? Your elementary classroom? How were the student desks and chairs arranged? Where was the teacher?

If you're like me, and I suspect many other people around the world, your classrooms probably included individual student desks (possibly with attached chairs), a teacher desk, a chalkboard or two, bookshelves full of encyclopedias and dictionaries, and probably a classroom library. If you were lucky, your teacher may have had an overhead projector and a television/VCR combination on a mobile cart. Most of your class time, especially in middle and high school, was probably spent sitting in your less-than-comfortable chair, listening to your teacher lecture while trying to find space on your desk for your textbook, notebook, and your writing arm. If you spoke during the instructional time, you were probably reprimanded. You would never have given listening to music on your portable CD player or Walkman a thought.

Does that sound familiar?

The classroom I described is not an archaic concept for many teachers and students. When I began my teaching career in August of 2008, my classroom included thirty individual student desks with attached chairs (Did anyone else hate those seats as much as I did as a student?), a teacher desk with desktop computer, a projector on a cart, and a DVD/VCR player I rented (more like hid in my classroom) from the library. As a new teacher, the thought of students talking to each other during class seemed like an encroachment on my instructional time, and I was offended! Looking back on my first year in the classroom, I have many "facepalm" moments where I wonder how I could have been so arrogant to think that I was this magical gatekeeper of knowledge and that my students could only learn information from my brain or our course textbook.

Wow, how times have changed!

Fortunately, I have realized that I am, in fact, not the gatekeeper of knowledge. My students don't (or shouldn't) need to rely on my knowledge of a concept to further their own understanding. Picture this: You bump into an individual at the grocery store who, for some reason, cannot remember the date that the Bill of Rights was ratified. They notice that you're a teacher, obviously, because your aura radiates compassion, love, a desire to positively impact the world, and sheer awesomeness. They run to you, seeking your knowledge of the Bill of Rights and ask, "When, oh fount of wisdom and knowledge, was the Bill of Rights ratified?"

Be honest. Unless you are a social studies teacher, American history guru, or have just happened to do a Google search for "Bill of Rights," your response will probably be one of two statements. You'll either respond with, "Uh, I'm not sure," as you politely scan the Gala apple selection, or you'll say, "Hang on, let me look that up."

If you were to ask my students that same question in my classroom today, they would either pull out their cell phones to ask Siri the question or do a quick Google search on their Chromebooks. Then they'll tell you that the Bill of Rights was ratified on December 15, 1791.

They can locate this information with or without me, their teacher. Am I the gatekeeper of these facts? Nope. What, then, is the role of the teacher?

I believe one of our jobs as teachers is to encourage students to emphasize the importance of collaboration and critical thinking. The marketplace our students will enter wants adults who can contribute to society by solving new problems and creating new solutions. The ability to regurgitate the date of an event, albeit an extremely important one, will likely not be helpful to our students; however, being able to apply the protections guaranteed by the Bill of Rights to modern issues while working with others is a valuable skill our students will undoubtedly need in their repertoire.

Teachers can use technology tools to design illuminating lessons that encourage students to collaborate and think critically with their peers—those in their classroom and in other parts of the world.

COLLABORATE AND THINK CRITICALLY WITH GOOGLE HANGOUTS

A favorite topic of discussion, especially in my American history classes, is "I wonder how people in other countries learn about _____." I always encourage my students to think about our history outside of how they've always learned it, and Google Hangouts offers the perfect tool for accomplishing this task!

As we were discussing the events that led to the American Revolutionary War, my students started talking about how they felt students in the United Kingdom may learn about this event. As the discussion was in full force, I asked, "Wouldn't it be neat to ask a student in England how they learn about the Revolutionary War?"

"*Yes!*" came the overwhelming response from my students.

As the class period ended, I shoved this discussion to the back of my mind and didn't think about it again until the next day, when my students asked if I had talked to anyone in England about the Revolutionary War yet.

I knew then that the idea of talking to someone in another country about world events was exciting to my students, and I had to make it happen.

I had recently attended a session at a conference about global collaborations. I was intrigued by this idea, but I didn't know how it would work in my classroom. To learn more, I contacted the presenter, who connected me with a teacher in the United Kingdom. We met via Google Hangout to discuss our plan for collaboration and to set up a timeline.

When I shared the plan with my students, they were excited! Right away, my class created a Padlet wall where each student shared an introductory post that included a picture or video, questions for the other students, and brief information about themselves. We shared the Padlet wall with the other class and received their introductory wall in return.

Learn more about global collaborations projects!
http://bit.ly/illuminate-global
#illuminateED

Students were able to create an amazing discussion through the Padlet wall that carried over into social media and our Google Hangout.

An issue with collaborating with other countries in real-time is, of course, time zone differences. My students willingly came to school at 6:30 in the morning to participate in the video call with students in the UK while they were at lunch. We talked about cultural stereotypes, college plans, favorite foods, Netflix, YouTube, and more. We ended our Hangout by playing an international game of Kahoot!.

This collaboration project has blossomed in my classroom, with my students now working with classes in Belgium and hopefully soon in other parts of the world. Global collaboration projects can encourage cultural empathy and awareness, which are essential to living and thriving in our global society.

Students and teachers can use global collaboration projects not only to introduce cultural differences and promote unity, but also to discuss global issues and how to solve them. Students in the United States, for example, may find it interesting to talk with classes in Europe about socialized medicine, weighing the pros and cons of each system.

USING G SUITE FOR EDUCATION TO COLLABORATE AND THINK CRITICALLY

When I was a senior in college, I was introduced to Google Docs, and yes, I know I'm dating myself. In my undergraduate technology for teachers' class, we learned how to use Google Docs and Google Sites and how they could be used in our future classrooms. As a die-hard Microsoft Office user, I was completely unimpressed with the plain, sometimes clunky Google Docs word processing tool. Innovation is the name of the game with Google; the transformation and expansion the Google suite of apps has experienced is nothing short of amazing.

Google tools have completely changed education for the better. G Suite tools like Drive, Docs, Sites, and Slides encourage increased communication and collaboration among students and teachers. Most of the work students submit in my class is through Google Classroom in the form of Google Docs or Slides. When they submit an assignment or project, I can evaluate their work and quickly provide them with feedback. Timely feedback is essential to learning because students can quickly determine whether or not they understand the content. Since these tools are cloud based, my students and I have the ability to access files on any computer, tablet, or smartphone.

When my students create presentations, they seem to prefer Google Slides as a creation tool. Can you blame them? Google Slides is great not only for creating presentations but for designing documents and images as well. Students can collaborate with each other to create stunning products that display their understanding of concepts. Students can work individually or in groups to create multiple presentations, or the teacher can create a single Google Slides presentation and allow students to add to and collaborate on a single presentation. In my classroom, we call the latter "single slide presentations," in which students (with or without a group) contribute to the final product. In these activities, each student creates his or her slide, adhering to project requirements. The individual slides are unique and creative, and really make the presentation awesome—all students are contributing to a class project. Single slide presentations and working with G Suite tools in general provide a great opportunity for peer review and feedback. If a student accidentally (or purposely) deletes a slide, changes a font, or somehow throws a wrench into the presentation, the revision history feature is available to calm fears and remedy the error.

Google Sites is also a great tool to encourage collaboration among students. Instead of creating a Google Slides presentation to demonstrate understanding of a topic, students can contribute to a class Google Site database; for example, students may be researching the impact of specific landmark Supreme Court cases on American history. Instead of creating a Google Slides presentation about this topic, students can contribute specific information to a Google Site that can be shared publicly (or privately) by the teacher. Sharing student work with an authentic audience can have a huge impact on the product students create. When students understand that their work will be shared with a large amount of people as opposed to only their teacher, they may be more likely to produce a higher caliber of work.

COLLABORATING AND THINKING CRITICALLY WITH FLIPGRID

Flipgrid is an excellent tool for encouraging critical thinking and collaboration. Students can make their case for or against any number of topics:

- Should the United States adopt a universal health care policy? Why or why not? Discuss evidence to support your claim.
- What is a problem in your community or school? How could you fix this problem?
- If you could create an app for your smartphone or tablet, what would it do?
- How should students be allowed or encouraged to use electronic devices in school?

Students can also participate in grids/topics with classes from other parts of the world. Imagine the conversations that can arise from these activities! Teachers can include topics like these:

- What is your favorite holiday to celebrate? Why? What traditions do you and your family have for this holiday?
- What are your favorite foods? What does your dinner table look like?
- How long is your school day? Do you go to school year-round?
- Where do you and your family go for vacation?

The conversations that come from these activities are amazing to behold. Students can collaborate with peers from other parts of the world to discuss everything from cultural stereotypes and misconceptions to global issues.

COLLABORATE AND THINK CRITICALLY WITH DIGITAL BREAKOUT EDU

"Breakout" or "escape" rooms have grown quite popular in recent years. And for good reason! There's the thrill of the hunt for clues, the excitement that rises when you achieve a task and can move to the next stage, and the sheer joy of finally solving the puzzle.

Breakout EDU puts an educational spin on characteristics of these breakout/escape rooms. Originally developed by Mark Hammons and James Sanders in 2015, Breakout EDU puzzles challenge students to work together and solve problems as they practice critical thinking skills. Appropriately difficult, these puzzles encourage students to "fail forward" and continue trying until their final lock opens, and they win!

The ability to "fail forward" is a skill our students desperately need to learn. When we decide to try something difficult or challenging, we rarely succeed on the first try. When I set out to run a 5K, I started by running short distances or for a small amount of time; I didn't hop on my treadmill and churn out 3.1 miles on day one. Was running difficult, at first? Yes, and honestly, it still is. Do I stop or give up because I didn't get it exactly right the first time? Nope.

Think back to when you learned to ride a bike. Most likely, you fell off your bike a few times or yelled at your parent to keep holding on so you didn't. Eventually, after trying and failing a few times, you figured it out. You learned to "fail forward" in acquiring a new skill. Yay for you!

Our students often fall short of the goal the first time they attempt something in our classroom. And when they fail, they're ready to throw in the towel. Breakout EDU activities encourage students to keep trying and work together until they solve the problem. And that's a

> Learning to fail forward will help our students develop the perseverance they need to achieve their goals.
>
> #ILLUMINATEED

skill our students will need to have in their toolbox when they leave our classrooms. Employers want employees who can innovate and think outside the box to solve problems. Learning to fail forward will help our students develop the perseverance they need to achieve their goals.

I like to use digital Breakout EDU activities as an opening activity or review activity for my students. I love watching my students practice valuable skills like collaborating with their peers, thinking critically to solve clues, communicating effectively, and failing forward.

Get Started with Breakout EDU

You can find traditional Breakout EDU games for your classroom at BreakoutEDU.com. That said, purchasing the games isn't always feasible for teachers. Or if you're like me, you learn about the concept of Breakout EDU at a conference on a Thursday afternoon and feel the need to immediately implement the activities in your classroom, only to find out that the kits are on backorder for a few weeks. (Note: Teachers can also create their own Breakout EDU kits using locks and boxes purchased from Amazon or most any home improvement store.)

As I was researching Breakout EDU activities to use in my classroom, I stumbled upon the concept of digital breakout activities. These digital activities, pioneered by Mari Venturino and Justin Birckbichler, allow teachers more freedom and flexibility with creating Breakout EDU activities for their students—and they're free.

You can use a number of different tools to create digital Breakout EDU activities for your students. For ideas, check out the "sandbox" on the Breakout EDU site (sites.google.com/site/digitalbreakoutjb/sandbox), join any of the many Facebook groups, or search other teachers' boards on Pinterest to find ready-to-use games.

I create a Google Site for each digital breakout I design and use a Google Form for the "locks" my students will open. Digital breakouts allow teachers to use multiple "locks" for their students; you're only limited by your imagination! A traditional Breakout EDU box includes physical locks, such as a directional lock, a three- or four-digit lock, a letter lock, and a lock with a small key. Teachers who create digital breakout activities can include many different locks, or the same type of lock throughout their game. The possibilities are endless.

Learn more about using Breakout EDU activities in your classroom! http://bit.ly/illuminate-breakout #illuminateED

Why, then, should you incorporate collaborative activities that challenge students to think critically in your classroom? In addition to a more engaging and exciting learning experience, students will develop and exercise skills that will prepare them for their futures. Working together is challenging, and it is a requirement in the world beyond school. Why shouldn't they practice this skill in our classrooms? Teachers can use technology tools to encourage their students to think critically about complex problems that plague our world today while collaborating with their peers both in their classroom and around the world.

Try This Tomorrow

Introduce a topic using a digital Breakout EDU activity. Create your own game using Google Sites and a variety of digital tools or use games created by other teachers by accessing sites.google.com/site/digitalbreakoutjb/sandbox. Share your ideas about using Breakout EDU activities with your students on Twitter!

#ILLUMINATEED

Learn more about how you can use technology tools to encourage your students to collaborate and think critically at usingeducationaltechnology.com/collaborate-think-critically.

Notes on Students Using Tech for
Collaboration and Critical Thinking

CHAPTER 6
ASSESSMENT WITH TECHNOLOGY

How do you assess student learning?
How can we use technology to enhance this process?

Think back to your time as a student. Did you like test days? Did your eyes light up at the opportunity to share what you had learned with your teacher? Could you contain your excitement when the teacher placed the Scantron form on your desk?

I bet you weren't overly enthusiastic.

Fortunately, in the twenty-first-century classroom, assessment doesn't *have* to be dull and boring. Thanks to some modern instructional technology tools, teachers can brighten assessment opportunities for their students by designing experiences that can be engaging, *effective*, and fun.

> ## Being a reflective teacher is essential to growing as a teacher.
> ### #ILLUMINATEED

Assessment, especially formative assessment, is vital to any classroom because it allows teachers to not only understand what their students have learned and what they need help with but also to evaluate their own teaching. Being a reflective teacher is essential to growing as a teacher. If we fail to evaluate our teaching and live in a false reality that our lessons are perfect, our content delivery is flawless, and we have no room to grow as educators, our students suffer! Technology tools empower us to gain a better understanding of student learning and to adjust our instruction to better meet their needs.

FORMATIVE ASSESSMENT WITH GOOGLE FORMS

Google really hit a home run when they created Forms. Google Forms can be used in so many different ways in the classroom, including (but not limited to) surveys, interest inventories, writing journals, Bell Ringers, and my favorite: formative assessment. One of the most amazing features of Google Forms is the ability to link the form data to a

Learn more about using Google Forms in your classroom!
http://bit.ly/illuminate-google-forms
#illuminateED

Google Sheet. This feature makes it easy to collect and store data from students on a spreadsheet. Add-ons for Sheets and Forms allow you to manage and analyze student assessment data.

When I use a Google Form as formative assessment, I use the conditional formatting option in the connected spreadsheet to create color-coded data to better visualize the results. By using the "quiz" feature in Forms, teachers can easily view student assessment results in the connected spreadsheet and can then create a color-coded system to represent student performance; for example, scores of 0–50 percent could be red in the spreadsheet, 51–79 percent could be yellow, and scores of 80 percent and above could be green.

Why these colors? Color-coding assessment data can allow teachers to quickly visualize student learning. Did most of your students score "red"? Maybe you need to re-teach that lesson! Did the majority of your students score "green"? Full speed ahead! Are you looking to

form groups for a project or activity? By using conditional formatting to create color-coded assessment results, teachers can quickly scan their spreadsheet to create effective groups.

GAME-BASED FORMATIVE ASSESSMENT

Let's face it. Completing assessments, whether formative or summative in nature, is probably not an all-time favorite for our students. Many students feel a huge sense of anxiety before an assess-

The unit assessment should
never be a surprise
for teachers or students.

#ILLUMINATEED

ment. Gamifying assessments helps alleviate some of that test anxiety by encouraging students to have fun while sharing what they've learned. Game-based formative assessment tools also provide teachers with fantastic feedback about their lesson by helping them visualize what students know, what content they need a little more help with, and the concepts with which our students are struggling. The unit assessment should never be a surprise for teachers or students. The following instructional technology tools can make assessment fun for students and teachers!

Kahoot! for Formative Assessment

When Kahoot! was released to the public in the late summer of 2013, it was—pardon the pun—a real game changer for classrooms. My building was in the beginning phases of adopting a 1:1 initiative and had started to encourage students to use personal devices for school purposes through a BYOD (bring your own device) program. I honestly cannot remember how I stumbled upon Kahoot!. I would typically credit my professional learning network on Twitter with such an amazing discovery, but I didn't join Twitter until February of 2014. Truth be told, I probably found Kahoot! while perusing the many Pinterest boards I follow.

I may not remember how I found this great tool, but my students definitely remember the fun experience this game helped to create in my classroom. As the wonderful Maya Angelou once said, "I've learned that people will forget what you said, people will forget what you did, but people will never forget how you made them feel." My students may not remember the course concepts they learned in my American government class, but I hope they remember a feeling of excitement and enjoyment of learning. Interactive tools like Kahoot! help me achieve that goal.

Get Started with Kahoot!

To get started using Kahoot! (kahoot.com) in your classroom, create a free account and search through thousands of ready-to-play kahoots that have been created by people all over the world.

If you're ready to create your own kahoot, simply select "New" and choose one of the four options. "Jumble" is new to Kahoot! and requires students to put information in the correct order instead of selecting a single correct response. The "Discussion" and "Survey" options are great for facilitating discussion and soliciting feedback. We use the "Quiz" option most frequently in my classroom to collect evidence of student learning.

Questions and responses for Kahoot! activities must be created within the confines of character counts. This challenge requires us to

Use Kahoot! Quizzes to . . .
- **Preview new material**
- **Assess student understanding**
- **Evaluate lesson effectiveness**
- **Engage students in content**
- **Make learning fun!**

craft concise and clear questions. Fortunately, Kahoot! guides us through the quiz creation process. When creating quizzes in Kahoot!, you can choose to include images (from Getty Images or uploaded) in the questions and game sign-in page, as well as display a YouTube video in the background as students are joining. As students answer questions in the game, they can view their score and rank on their own devices and can see the class leaderboard on the board in the front of the room. Only the top five competitors are listed on the leaderboard, which can motivate your students to answer questions correctly.

Students join the game by entering a code provided by the teacher and a nickname for themselves. (Note: Teachers can kick students out of the game if their nicknames are less than appropriate.) When everyone has joined the game, a question is displayed on the board connected to the teacher's computer along with answer choices. The answer choices are shown in different colored boxes that also include a shape. On their devices, the students see the colored box and shape without the question. After students have completed each question (or time for that question has expired), a bar graph

Learn more about using Kahoot!
in your classroom!
http://bit.ly/illuminate-kahoot
#illuminateED

is displayed on the screen that shows the number of questions that have been answered correctly and incorrectly. Teachers can use this information to immediately review the content with students. Students of all ages love using Kahoot! to share their understanding of content.

Quizizz for Formative Assessment

As I shared in Chapter 3, students love memes. Really, who doesn't love a good meme? Memes can be a fun addition to your classroom, and Quizizz helps you make it happen. As students participate in Quizizz games, they are presented with memes depending on the accuracy of their responses.

Quizizz is a free tool that, like Kahoot!, encourages students to share what they've learned in a fun and engaging way. Teachers can create their own games to use with students (with no limit to character counts) or can use games created by others. Unlike Kahoot!, Quizizz allows teachers to insert individual questions (or quizzes) created by other teachers into their activities. I've found that this can be extremely helpful for my students. Sometimes our students can grow so accustomed to our question-writing style that they may not be able to apply concepts they've learned if a question is asked differently. Using questions from other teachers ensures that they have the content, not just the right answers for our questions.

When creating activities with Quizizz, teachers can include up to four response options and one correct answer. Questions can include subscript and superscript information, multiple text colors, and math, Greek, Latin, or currency symbols. Teachers can choose to play their game in class or can assign Quizizz activities to students as homework by link, through social media, or Google Classroom. Teachers can also create collections of Quizizz activities and can add games to any collection.

Students access the Quizizz activity just as they would a Kahoot! game—through a code/pin provided by the teacher and username. Quizizz also allows you to share and/or assign the game through Google Classroom, in which case students do not need a pin to join the game. If they join through Classroom, students will be asked to log in with their Google account information and then enter their name. This option is ideal for younger students.

When students join the Quizizz game, they will be assigned a randomly selected avatar, which cannot be changed. The avatars are quite silly, and it's fun for everyone to see what avatar they are assigned. As students join the game, their names and avatars are displayed on the board. As with Kahoot!, teach-ers have the ability to remove students from the game if their display names are, shall we say, less than appropriate.

Many students appreciate that the Quizizz game ques-tions and answer options are displayed on their individual computers as opposed to the whiteboard. While students are playing the game, their progress is displayed on the teacher's screen. Teachers can view individual student progress, includ-ing how many questions the students have answered correctly and incor-rectly as well as how many questions are unanswered. Teachers can also view how the entire class responded to individual questions; they're even color-coded. This can be extremely helpful during a previewing activity

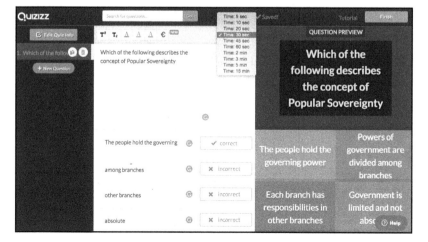

and formative assessment, as it allows you to see, at a glance, if the class is "getting" the concept or if more review is necessary.

As students answer questions, they earn points based on speed and accuracy of their response. When they complete each question, they are greeted with a meme based on whether their answer  was correct. I love this feature! It's one more way Quizizz helps make formative assessment fun!

Quizlet Live for Formative Assessment

Perhaps you're already familiar with the online flashcard site, Quizlet. But there is so much more to Quizlet than flashcards. A few years ago, Quizlet unveiled Quizlet Live, a fun review activity that requires students to work together with their classmates to answer content-related questions.

One of the many reasons I like Quizlet Live is that it promotes mastery learning. Students are unable to "win" unless they correctly answer eleven questions in a row. These questions are taken from flashcard decks chosen by the teacher. These decks can be created by students, teachers, or anyone who has access to Quizlet.

To get started, teachers access their account and select a flashcard deck. After opening the deck, teachers will see a variety of review options, including more traditional activities such as "flashcards" or "test" as well as "match" and "gravity," which are fun and competitive games. A favorite in my classroom is "match," which encourages students to match words with definitions quickly and accurately. "Match" also keeps track of who has completed the game in the best time, which quickly becomes a race to see who can finish the game faster than Mrs. Petty!

By selecting "live," teachers can launch a class game from a flashcard deck in a matter of seconds. Students join the game with a pin by accessing the Quizlet Live (quizlet.live) and entering their name. My students enjoy using their gamertag for this and other formative assessment games instead of their given name.

At least six students must join for the game to begin. When all students have joined, the teacher starts the game, and students are randomly sorted into teams. (If you purchase the premium version of Quizlet, you can create your own teams.) Each team is represented by an animal mascot. My students love this feature! We've had teams led by mythical unicorns, dragons, majestic eagles, and mighty bears. It's fun!

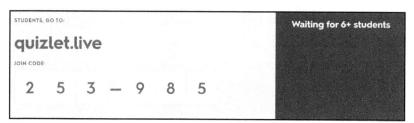

When the game begins, each student (all students participating must have a device) in the group sees a question displayed on their device as well as columns of answers. They can view the answer options on their answer column but are unable to view the response choices of their teammates. The team must work together to choose the correct answer. If they continue to answer questions correctly, their team advances across the board. If they answer a question incorrectly, they start the game from the beginning. This important feature of Quizlet Live both encourages student collaboration and requires students to review content material they miss.

Quizalize for Formative Assessment

Like the Google Forms/Spreadsheet example above, Quizalize allows teachers to visualize student learning. Using this free tool, teachers can easily create fun formative assessment activities for their students. Teachers create a free account and can even sync their Google Classroom roster with Quizalize to make assigning activities much easier. As students complete the activity, you can view in real-time where students need help and which students are struggling or excelling. Teachers can include images for questions, select a variety of time limits for answering questions, provide explanations for correct answers, and even include math functions in questions and responses.

Learn more about using Quizalize in your classroom! http://bit.ly/illuminate-quizalize #illuminateED

Similar to Kahoot! or Quizizz, Quizalize activities are competitive and fun, with students earning points for accuracy and speed in answering questions.

Adding games to your classroom can enhance the learning environment and help to increase student engagement! Think about it: Would you rather complete a Scantron test or play Kahoot!? I think we know the answer.

Wizer.Me for Assessment

I hesitate to call Wizer an online worksheet creator, because worksheets are bland, dull, boring, and stagnant. Wizer is anything *but* these things! Using Wizer (Wizer.Me), you can create interactive assignments that incorporate discussions, multiple-choice questions, videos, charts, and more. You can then assign the activity to students through Google Classroom, link, or a learning-management system, and can turn off access to the assignment at any time. Wizer also listens to teacher feedback—which is extremely important for any instructional technology tool—and frequently asks teachers to vote on new features. The features with the most votes are added to Wizer. It's fantastic!

Learn more about using Wizer.Me in your classroom! http://bit.ly/illuminate-wizer #illuminateED

By using technology tools like those discussed in this chapter to design and administer formative and summative assessments, you can offer students quality assessments and use the data to effectively reflect upon your lessons and units, design informed instruction, and provide quick feedback to students. All of which lead to a more effective learning environment. Go for it!

Try This Tomorrow

Search public Quizizz games created by other teachers by accessing quizizz.com. Teachers can choose to play existing games and can also select questions from games created by others to use in their activity. Share your experience with Quizizz on Twitter!

#ILLUMINATEED

Learn more about using technology tools to assess student learning at usingeducationaltechnology.com/assessing.

Notes on Assessing with Tech

CHAPTER 7
REFLECTING WITH TECHNOLOGY

How can we encourage our students to reflect upon their understanding?

Student reflection is important and all too often overlooked. Just as teachers should evaluate and reflect upon their teaching, students should be given the opportunity to reflect upon what they have learned, what they don't understand, how they contributed to a discussion, activity, or project, and what they can do to improve.

After completing a unit HyperDoc, my students reflect upon what they have learned through the unit, how well they participated in the unit activities, and what they can do to have a more effective learning

> When students recognize the importance of their role in the learning process, they become more engaged and empowered learners.
>
> #ILLUMINATEED

experience in the future. Their reflection also includes their feelings about how the material was presented and what I could do differently in future units to serve them better. Their reflections are extremely helpful for me, specifically those concerning their participation and effort as well as how the activities and presentation helped their learning. I have redesigned unit activities, bonus opportunities, and formative assessment based on these reflections. Reflection is key to growth! When students recognize the importance of their role in the learning process, they become more engaged and empowered learners.

REFLECTING WITH PADLET

I've already mentioned a few of the ways I use Padlet in my classroom to share ideas, promote collaboration, and introduce topics. Another way I use Padlet in my in-class flip is as a reflection tool for my students. As students view videos and create content, they progress through course units at different paces. Although I love that they can move at their own speed, it can make it difficult for me to keep track of what content the class needs to review or revisit.

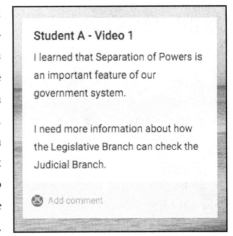

Here's where Padlet comes in. I create a Padlet wall for each unit for each section I teach, and I post this Padlet in the *About* portion of each section of Google Classroom. As students complete instructional videos and course activities, they post their thoughts and reflections in this collaborative space. The requirements for these posts vary but always include this instruction: "List *at least* one thing you learned from this activity and one thing you need more explanation on."

Students continually post to this wall throughout the unit. This provides a great resource for students and a space for discussion with the addition of the commenting feature on Padlet. At the end of the unit, I can also create a screencast of the Padlet wall using Screencastify and share that video on YouTube or through Google Drive. This gives my students a review video specific to what they need.

REFLECTING THROUGH CREATING

One of my many goals as a teacher is to offer my students *choice* when it comes to presenting and reflecting on their knowledge. Some students may prefer to share what they've learned in an essay, others may excel at creating videos, while some may enjoy writing a song or creating an infographic. The possibilities are endless. I want students to create representations of their knowledge in my class, not just consume information. I also don't want to force students to show what they've learned in one specific, cookie-cutter way. We don't live in a one-size-fits-all world today even though standardized tests are still prevalent throughout the realm of education. We should encourage students to create representations of their knowledge instead of completing dry and boring worksheets.

One of my favorite takeaways from *The HyperDoc Handbook* (other than HyperDocs themselves, of course) was the concept of a "Show What You Know" Bingo. I use this concept in all my HyperDocs, and my students appreciate the fact that they can choose how they want to share their understanding.

"Show What You Know Bingo" was developed by Lisa Highfill, Kelly Hilton, and Sarah Landis. This concept has been modified by Bethany Petty.

Some students love creating videos. Others thrive on writing essays. Some students prefer to create visuals of their learning. Teachers can design learning experiences that provide students with choices in how they reflect upon their learning by utilizing instructional technology tools.

REFLECTING WITH FLIPGRID

As with Padlet, I've already mentioned a few ideas for using Flipgrid that allow you to collect video evidence of student learning. It's also an excellent tool for student reflection and can be used in the following ways:

Class Discussions

My students frequently participate in online discussion forums in which they analyze primary and secondary sources, respond to questions/prompts, and then reflect upon and discuss their ideas with their classmates in this online environment. Flipgrid can supplement (or replace) written discussion board activities and can encourage students to share their opinions and ideas verbally.

Book Reviews, Analysis, or Recommendations

Do your students read novels for your class? Students can provide their analysis and review of books with Flipgrid. You can share student video responses through link, embed code, Google Classroom, social media, or through a QR Code that can be posted anywhere.

Exit Tickets

Assign Flipgrid topics as exit tickets at the end of a lesson, activity, or unit to encourage students to reflect upon their learning. You and your students can comment on videos to answer remaining questions they have about the content. They can also ask additional questions and contribute to meaningful conversations about the content through video.

REFLECTING THROUGH GOOGLE FORMS

Google Forms can be used in a multitude of ways in the classroom, one of which is to encourage students to reflect on their learning experiences.

At the end of each unit, before the assessment, my students complete a Google Form reflection that focuses on a few main points: content knowledge, learning experience and commitment, and what we can change to make the next unit even better.

Content Knowledge

One of the chief goals of each unit is obviously to learn and gain a deeper understanding of our content. The first section of the Google Form reflection that my students complete includes a few questions that come from each instructional video in the unit. This encourages students to review content information and provides me with excellent formative assessment data. One of the many perks of using Google Forms to collect evidence of student learning is that the data are deposited into a Google Sheet. Teachers can use a variety of tools within the spreadsheet to view and analyze data, but my favorite tool is color coding using conditional formatting (as discussed in Chapter 6) that allows me to quickly see which and how many students understand or are struggling with the content.

Learning Experience and Commitment

As students finish a unit or a project, it's extremely important for them to reflect upon and think about what they learned, how the learning experience worked for them, and how committed they were to their learning. Students respond to questions that focus on the knowledge they acquired throughout the unit as well as how the learning experiences helped them learn the content. Through metacognitive activities designed to promote student reflection, students are encouraged to become more efficient and focused in their learning.

How Can We Enhance Your Learning?

This is my favorite part of the Google Form reflection because I really feel like I'm gaining insight into how my students view our classroom and how we can make it better. The reflection piece allows me to understand how my students perceive our class. My students have shared brilliant

> Our students are the reason we do what we do. Why shouldn't we include them in the process of designing their learning experiences?
>
> #ILLUMINATEED

insights with me about my courses, and as I review their feedback, I am better able to design learning experiences that truly reach my students. Our students are the reason we do what we do. Why shouldn't we include them in the process of designing their learning experiences?

REFLECTING WITH FLIPPITY

I found Flippity a few years ago while searching for an online flashcard creator. I appreciate the simplicity Flippity offers and how easily students can create a flashcard set. The program allows students to save their flashcards on their Google Drive by simply accessing the Flippity site and making a copy of a Google Sheet. This feature means students always have access to their work even if they can't find the URL for their flashcards.

But Flippity is much more than a flashcard generator. Students and teachers can also use Flippity to create the following reflection and review tools:

- Game-Show-style Review Games
- Memory/Matching Games
- Crossword Puzzles
- Word Searches

- Tournament Brackets
- Hangman-style Games
- Mix-and-Match Games

While these activities can be extremely helpful when they are created by teachers to be used in review, Flippity can also be a powerful tool for students to use to reflect on their knowledge. Teachers can encourage students to use Flippity to create review stations for their peers in the middle of a unit or in preparation for an assessment. Teachers and students can create QR codes that direct to their Flippity activities and post these codes throughout the classroom.

Reflection is extraordinarily important for growth for teachers and students alike. When we provide students with opportunities to choose how they demonstrate their understanding of concepts, our students can become more engaged and invested in the success of the final product. Encouraging students to not only become involved in the content of your course but also to take an interest in how they are learning can be very powerful.

Try This Tomorrow

Sign up for a Padlet account at padlet.com and create a "wall of reflection" for your students. Encourage your students to use this wall as an exit ticket after they complete a learning activity. Use this wall to design review activities (such as instructional videos) and to determine the content on which students need more instruction. Share your experiences on Twitter!

#ILLUMINATEED

Learn more about how you can encourage your students to use technology to reflect at usingeducationaltechnology.com/reflect.

Note

Lisa Highfill, Kelly Hilton, and Sarah Landis, *The HyperDoc Handbook* (EdTechTeam Press, 2016).

Notes on Reflecting with Technology

Chapter 8
Motivate with Technology

What motivated you as a student?
How do you encourage and motivate students to succeed in your classroom?
How do you use technology to motivate and encourage your students?

At some point in our lives, we all experience the pangs of having no motivation to complete a task. I am unmotivated daily to keep my house clean; just ask my husband. We've also all felt the excitement and momentum of being motivated to do something. The rush of creating a product, sharing an experience, or finishing a project is a wonderful feeling and can propel us and our students to greatness. Motivation is essential to being successful in any endeavor.

What motivated you as a student? Was it earning an *A* in a class? Was it making your parents proud of your accomplishments? Was it that sense of achievement that welled up inside your chest when you finished a project into which you had poured your heart and soul?

As a student, I was certainly motivated by some of those feelings. I loved to see the pride in my parents' faces when I showed them a report card filled with *A*'s. I grew up in a household where excelling in school was important, and this emphasis on academics was enough to motivate me to learn as much as I could while in school. I learned that working hard and trying my best was essential to being successful in the classroom and in the "real world." When I completed online courses in my undergraduate degree program, the learning-management system we used allowed the instructor to select a graduation cap icon on student responses to discussion boards. This meant that the particular statement had been evaluated by the teacher and had been deemed exemplary.

All the students in the class could see this icon. At the end of every week, I would frantically access my response to see if it had earned the endorsement of the instructor.

I was motivated to succeed and push myself to excel in school because I wanted to do so. My home environment encouraged this motivation in me. You may not have had this same experience. Our students may not have this type of home life. They may be motivated by other factors. Our job is to figure out how to motivate our students and encourage them to be excited about learning, creating, sharing, and working together in our classroom and the world beyond school.

How can we encourage and motivate our students to reach their full potential—not only in our classrooms but in their lives? How can we get them *excited* to learn while they work together to understand and apply concepts? I have a few ideas . . .

MOTIVATING STUDENTS WITH YOUTUBE

In February of 2005, the world was forever changed when YouTube sprang into action. My daughters have never known a world without YouTube. Today's students have grown up with YouTube. They use it to listen to music, learn about virtually anything, watch funny movies, and, if they're like my daughters, watch toy-unboxing videos.

YouTube has the potential to be an amazing learning tool. Teachers can use it to create content for students, students can create content for anyone, and videos can be accessed almost anywhere.

I think it's unfortunate that YouTube is blocked in many schools where teachers, the leadership, or perhaps the community fear students will stumble onto (or actively search for) inappropriate content. Of course, negative and inappropriate videos and comments exist on YouTube, but should we as educators prevent our students from using this tool because of a few *"bad apples"*? I say, "No way!" Schools can also utilize filtering options for YouTube use to limit the possibility of inappropriate content being displayed. The YouTube Kids app is also available for Android and iOS devices, which provides a variety of parental control options.

When I created and uploaded my first instructional video to YouTube, I was terrified. Why? Because everyone in the world was going to have the ability to view my video. I worried about how I sounded, what I said, and how I said it. I recorded and rerecorded my video more times than I care to admit, and when I finally published my video on YouTube, I continually refreshed the page for the rest of the evening, waiting and watching for views, likes, and comments. Now I use Screencastify to create instructional videos for my students in my flipped American government classes and post them on my YouTube channel on a regular basis.

Our students have grown up surrounded by social media. They like, retweet, and comment on images, videos, and posts as if doing so is second nature. And unlike me when I posted my first video, our students are comfortable sharing online as well. It's time to use this to our advantage in education. While it's true that students may not feel as nervous as their teachers might when sharing videos, neither do they do so flippantly. When students create videos to share on YouTube (or other video services), they tend to focus on producing quality content. Why? Because they know others will take the opportunity to give them a thumbs up (or down), and they do not want to share

> ## Students Can Create Videos to . . .
>
> - Explain a landmark Supreme Court case
> - Demonstrate a science experiment
> - Review a book or text
> - Explain a concept
> - Present a project
> - Model how to solve a math problem
> - Demonstrate a process

garbage on the internet. Once again, an authentic audience motivates them to put their best effort into their work.

Flipped-classroom teachers likely create dozens of videos for their students. The majority of these videos are instructional in nature and describe a course concept, project, process, etc. Teachers can also harness the power of video creation to encourage and motivate their students to succeed using humor!

When I started flipping my classroom, my videos were 100 percent focused on delivering content in a compact package on YouTube. I found that I could present a lesson that would have taken me an entire fifty-minute class period in a traditional lecture environment in about four minutes. It's fantastic. I also found, however, that my students were still struggling with some of our course concepts. One day I was exasperated and frustrated that my students weren't "getting" the concept of federalism. Instead of throwing up my hands and giving up, I said, "Maybe I should just rap about it," and then chuckled. I did not expect my students to say, "Yes!!" I was dumbfounded. I can't rap! I can barely sing! But I shed my dignity and created what I thought was a truly horrible "freestyle rap" about the fabulous concept of federalism. The response? My students loved it. They asked for an encore and then told me to put it on YouTube. They were completely shocked when I said, "I will!"

Then I actually did it. This was the day my alter ego, Petty Wap, was born.

Since uploading my original "rap," I've added more than a dozen "beats" to my Petty Wap YouTube playlist. Yes, my students bestowed upon me the name "Petty Wap" and frequently refer to me by that name. Being willing to be silly and add some fun to our class has helped me forge great relationships with my students. It helped me to help them connect with the content I'm teaching and motivate them in my classroom. If I can encourage them to be excited about my class and motivate them to do their best by acting a little strange, so be it. I've donned sock caps, danced, done toe-touches, and have promised a wig and maybe some chainmail in the future. Your students will love seeing your excitement not only for your content, but for their learning. Shed your shame and infuse your classroom with humor. It's fun!

When my students get "stuck" on a course concept, we stop and make a rap about it. Sometimes we may devote more class time than I would like to creating these raps, but it's not about what I want. My classroom is a learning environment for my students.

MOTIVATING STUDENTS THROUGH GAMIFICATION

A few years ago, our district had an unbelievable winter with twenty snow days. Twenty! That's unheard of, and it's far more than the number of planned make-up days, so many of the snow days were added to the end of the school year. When teachers and students are accustomed to releasing for the summer in early May and find themselves still in session closer to June, school can get a little *blah*.

Fourth quarter of that school year was, and I hate to use this term, brutal. Motivation on both sides of the desk sank to an all-time low, and I was desperate to find an activity or strategy that would encourage and motivate everyone in the classroom (myself included) to continue to be productive instead of slipping into a funk. I thought back through some of the professional development I had been to that school year and remembered what I'd learned about gamification at a conference. Although I found the strategy intriguing, I had pushed gamification to the back burner because I didn't understand how it could fit with my content area.

Bad idea.

Gamification is a great motivational strategy that applies gaming concepts to the classroom. I must confess: Until I learned about gamification in the classroom, "gaming," to my mind, meant playing *Super Mario Brothers* on my Nintendo and calling "all-time Mario," which forced my younger sister to wait quite some time to actually play. (I was awesome back in the nineties.) The experience kids have playing modern video games is quite different from what I experienced as Player 1 on *Super Mario Brothers*. Games today allow students to earn experience points (often called XP) and badges, go on quests, achieve objectives, level up or evolve, succeed and fail, and keep trying until they beat the game. Gamifiying your classroom is all about incorporating those elements into your course.

Put yourself in your students' shoes. How fun would it be to participate in class activities (instructional videos, discussion boards, projects, etc.) and earn XP that allows you to level up and earn "tools" to use in the class? What if you earn an outstanding score on your assessment? Would receiving a badge to display on your workspace motivate you to try harder, especially if you didn't care about the actual grade you earn? Think about the idea of completing "objectives" to earn "XP" to help you "level up" and acquire "tools" to use on your mission instead of simply completing classwork to get a grade.

The first scenario sounds a little more fun, right?

If you're like me, the concept of gamification may seem a bit daunting. Never fear! To get started with gamification in your classroom, ask yourself a few questions:

- How will my students earn points (XP [experience points], team points, academic points, etc.)?
- What will XP do for them?
- Will my students level up?
- How will my students visualize their "level?"

In my classroom, "Mission: American Government" is a multifaceted "game" designed to encourage students to engage in instructional activities and assignments and to go above and beyond requirements to explore and analyze content in a way that creates a more thorough understanding of course concepts.

Students earn XP by . . .

- Completing course assignments ON TIME
- Participating in activities

Students earn Bonus XP by . . .

- Completing "bonus missions" (extra credit or independent study)
- Finishing in the top five in review activities (Kahoot!, Quizizz, etc.)
- General awesomeness

Students use the XP they earn to "level up," which allows them to use "tools" (in gaming lingo, tools are often called weapons, but I don't like using that terminology in my classroom) on their unit assessment. The image below shows a few of the levels I use along with the XP required to reach each level.

	Bronze (50-300)	Silver (301-500)	Gold (501-700)	Ruby (701-900)
Candy	Small candy on test day	Small candy on test day	Small candy bar on test day	Small candy bar on test day
Bonus Points	x	2	2	3
50/50	x	x	x	x
Post-It	x	x	x	x

At the beginning of the year, I put a "gamertag" form in the "About" section of Google Classroom. My students complete this form by including a school-appropriate nickname for our game, which is displayed on our "leaderboard" alongside their XP total. I create a Google Sheet for each of my class sections, share that spreadsheet with each class via Google Classroom, and then use conditional formatting to help students visualize what level they and their classmates have reached.

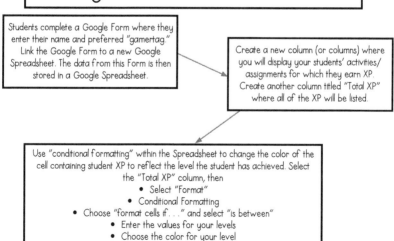

Getting Started with Gamification

Students complete a Google Form where they enter their name and preferred "gamertag." Link the Google Form to a new Google Spreadsheet. The data from this Form is then stored in a Google Spreadsheet.

Create a new column (or columns) where you will display your students' activities/assignments for which they earn XP. Create another column titled "Total XP" where all of the XP will be listed.

Use "conditional formatting" within the Spreadsheet to change the color of the cell containing student XP to reflect the level the student has achieved. Select the "Total XP" column, then
- Select "Format"
  - Conditional Formatting
- Choose "format cells if . . ." and select "is between"
  - Enter the values for your levels
  - Choose the color for your level
- Add additional "rules" for your levels

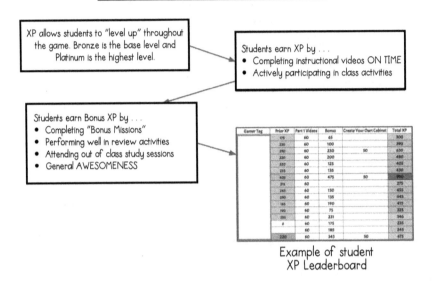

Example of student
XP Leaderboard

Gamification can take many forms in the classroom. Think back to the token economy your elementary school classrooms may have utilized. As a student, you may have earned stickers, play money, or actual tokens, and when you had amassed a specific amount, you could go to the "treasure chest" to select a prize.

Gamifying your classroom—adding game elements to your classroom activities and assignments—may seem like a foreign concept, especially if you're like me and are almost completely unfamiliar with the world of gaming. If, however, offering XP or Bonus XP to your students for completing tasks and allowing them to use their XP to reach new levels and earn tools to use on an assessment motivates your students and encourages them to succeed, so be it! Using technology to gamify classroom activities could be the light bulb students need to motivate them to succeed.

MOTIVATING STUDENTS THROUGH COMMUNICATION

Technology tools have made sharing information easier than ever before. Communicating with our students and their parents/guardians is essential and can be a great motivator for our students because they know the lines of communication are open and freely flowing between their teacher and their parents.

Communicating with Remind

I started using Remind about three years ago, and it is definitely one of my favorite tech tools for classroom communication. At the beginning of the school year, I post a QR code on my "important information" bulletin board that takes students and parents to the link where they can join Remind for each of my classes. I use Remind to send announcements, reminders, bonus opportunities, current events information, content review information, videos, articles, and anything else that is relevant to my students. I love being able to send these announcements and messages to my students in a safe, documented text message (without sharing my personal phone number). I use Remind as a Twitter-like tool in which my students and I can communicate more efficiently than email. Let's face it; our students are more likely to check a text message than an email! Remind is not a one-way messaging service, or at least it doesn't *have* to be. Remind offers teachers, coaches, administrators, etc. the ability to send and receive direct messages from their students.

Communicating with Google Classroom

Recently, Google added a feature to allow parents/guardians to receive periodic summaries of their student's progress through Google Classroom. With more and more teachers utilizing Google Classroom as a document-management system, the ability for parents/guardians to view their student's assignments helps promote open lines of communication between parents, students, and teachers! To utilize this feature, teachers can enter parents'/guardians' email addresses for their students. Parents/guardians will then receive daily or weekly email summaries of their student's work.

Communicating through Google Sites

Google Sites allows you to create an informative class website that you can share with students' parents and the community. With the recent updates to Sites, you can easily drag and drop content blocks (text, images, embed codes, files from computer or Google Drive) into your site and create multiple pages to share information. Simplify sharing by putting everything in one place; for example, you can embed your Google Classroom calendar on your Google Site to be sure parents have access to due dates and upcoming events.

ENCOURAGEMENT—A GREAT MOTIVATOR

While encouraging our students may seem like an obvious motivator and may appear to have nothing to do with instructional technology, it is an essential component of an effective classroom. I, like many of you, have had students enter my classroom with their mind already made up about teachers and school. Some may believe that their teachers don't really care about them as people and are only concerned with how well they perform on a standardized test. As a teacher, one of my foundational goals is that my students know I care about them as individuals and that I want to see them succeed not only in my class but also in life.

I want to encourage my students to continue to persevere even in the face of failure. If they submit an assignment that doesn't meet the standard, I want them to "redo" their work. I return the assignment to them through Google Classroom with specific comments and encourage them to try again. If plain ol' encouragement doesn't motivate them to try again, I may even throw in some Bonus XP upon completion of the assignment. Above all, I want my students to understand that I'm not returning an assignment to them to redo because I'm "nitpicking" at their work or because I'm trying to create more work for them. I want them to realize that they *can* create amazing products, and that I am in their corner, cheering them on!

One way I encourage and inspire my students is through my "take what you need" bulletin board. The truth is, students often feel overwhelmed with school, sports, jobs, and home lives and can use

I want them to realize that they *can* create amazing products, and that I am in their corner, cheering them on!
#ILLUMINATEED

a pick-me-up throughout the day. My "take what you need" board includes inspirational quotes and sayings on small pieces of paper that are stapled to the board for students to take when they feel stressed, worried, or when they just need a smile. I've found that my students will take phrases from the board not only for themselves, but also for their peers who may need some positivity. I've refilled this board many times, which speaks volumes to the message I hoped to convey.

When students realize that their teacher cares about their success and growth, and not only about their performance on standardized tests, they become more engaged in their learning. By trying a new motivation or encouragement strategy with your students, you're letting them know you care!

Create your own
"Take What You Need" bulletin
board in your classroom!
http://bit.ly/illuminate-encourage
#illuminateED

Try This Tomorrow

Create a free Remind account, set up classes, and encourage your students and their parents to join. Use Remind to alert parents and students to upcoming classroom events, activities, assignments, and tests. Encourage parents and students to correspond with you through this Remind account!

#illuminateED

Learn more about how you can use technology to motivate your students at usingeducationaltechnology.com/motivate.

Notes on Motivating Students with Tech

Chapter 9
Designing Lessons with Technology

How can we use technology to design lessons and units that enhance the learning environment?

When I started teaching in August of 2008, I immediately fell in love with creating lessons and designing units. Yes, of course I fell in love with teaching too! Call me a nerd if you want, but the process of reading the standards, locating and curating resources, creating assessments, designing activities, and collecting evidence of student learning is just so fun! Technology tools have made this process even better and allow students to achieve the Four Cs of twenty-first-century learning in so many ways.

DESIGNING LESSONS WITH HYPERDOCS

Lisa Highfill, Kelly Hilton, and Sarah Landis developed and shared the concept of HyperDocs because they were looking for a way to fully utilize the power of Google tools in the classroom to create a more personalized learning experience for their students. In their book, *The HyperDoc Handbook*, these authors share a variety of lesson and unit templates and activities to encourage students to dive deeper into the content of their lesson and expand their understanding of course concepts.

There are *many* ways to design a lesson or unit using the HyperDoc model. *The HyperDoc Handbook* (and accompanying website) provides teachers with awesome starting points for designing engaging lessons for students using technology tools. The variety of templates the authors offer makes it easy to create an effective HyperDoc. I also like to create my own HyperDocs based on my students' specific needs.

That's part of the beauty of the HyperDoc model—there is no one way to do it!

One of my favorite characteristics of HyperDocs is the flexibility that it brings to lesson and unit planning. *The HyperDoc Handbook* authors identify many elements that go into designing lessons and provide great examples of tools that teachers include in their lesson. While every HyperDoc may not follow the same pattern, most will probably include similar elements that may include the following:

- Engage
- Explore
- Explain
- Apply
- Reflect
- Share
- Extend

The first part of lesson planning for me is including an element designed to **engage** students in the content of our lesson or unit. If we dive into the US Constitution without a hook to get students excited

---

Economic Theories
Mini **HYPERDOC**

Explore

Preview Market, Traditional, Command, and Mixed Economies with this game

Explain

Please read this article about the three main economic systems.

Create a copy of this document to record your notes on the article.

Apply

Click here to complete the Form for this assignment

Reflect

Access the Economic Theories Padlet and follow the instructions on the site

Extend

Using Google and (NEW!) Google Earth, locate and explore countries that utilize command and mixed market economies.

---

about the content of our unit, they'll most likely view the Constitution as words written on a really old piece of paper instead of the exciting, influential, and foundational concepts it holds. I love including YouTube videos, images, or content-related games in this part of my HyperDocs to pull my students into the content of our lesson or unit, essentially using technology to illuminate the path of learning.

Many HyperDocs will also include an **explore** section designed to encourage students to access supplemental information about the content of the lesson or unit. One of my favorite tools to use in this section of my HyperDocs is Google Earth! Using my Constitution unit as an example, imagine the level of interest your students will have in using a fun tool like Google Earth to visit historic buildings and places associated with the creation and signing of the Constitution. This activity will probably be more exciting than looking at pictures in a textbook.

Engage and explore sections can be used interchangeably, together, and in a different order in your HyperDoc. That flexibility in lesson planning is a huge perk to design.

The **explain** section of my HyperDocs normally includes a link to Edpuzzle, where my students sign in to their account and view instructional videos. Some of my HyperDocs include links to articles or other resources where my students can find information about our content. This section of my HyperDoc also includes instructions or reminders for note-taking. (My students normally take notes on content on a Google Doc that I share with them through Google Classroom.) This section also includes a brief activity that encourages students to **reflect** upon what they've learned and what they need help with.

The **apply** element is the section of the HyperDoc that has been most transformational for my lessons. When I started teaching, I would typically ask students to apply their knowledge of my content through a worksheet. With the availability of technology tools, I can provide my students with the opportunity to create and share amazing products while offering them *choice* in how to demonstrate their knowledge. Some students prefer to create a screencast to demonstrate their understanding of a topic. Many of my students share my love for writing, while others may prefer to create an infographic to display their understanding of a concept. When students are given choices of how they want to share what they've learned, the quality of work they produce tends to improve because they feel a sense of ownership in the project.

I've noted the importance of taking time to **reflect** upon learning. A reflection element can be woven into other steps of a HyperDoc or can be a stand-alone piece of the activity. Students can use a unit study guide

> When students are given choices of how they want to share what they've learned, the quality of work they produce tends to improve because they feel a sense of ownership in the project.
>
> **#ILLUMINATEED**

as a tool for reflection as well as preparing and reviewing for an assessment. Students can use a Padlet wall, Google Form, table within the Google Doc (Slide, Site, Form, or whatever packaging tool you choose!), or a game-based formative assessment tool to reflect upon the content of the lesson or unit.

Depending on the HyperDoc, teachers can include an option for students to **share** what they've learned or created with their peers or a wider audience. I've found that when students realize their work may be seen by someone other than their teacher for grading purposes, they will more than likely create a more quality product. Creating work for authentic audiences is powerful.

The **extend** element of HyperDocs can be extremely powerful for students because it can encourage them to continue learning about a topic beyond what their lesson or unit has required. I've found that including "Bonus Missions" (See Chapter 8 for more on gamification!)

as part of this section is great for students who want to go above and beyond what's expected!

HyperDoc Tools

Here are a few of my favorite tools you can include for each element of a HyperDoc:

Engage
→ YouTube
→ Podcasts
→ Canva
→ Adobe Spark
→ Memes

Explore
→ Google Earth
→ Google Maps

Explain
→ EDpuzzle
→ Nearpod
→ Text relevant to your topic

Apply
→ Screencasts with Screencastify
→ Blog Post through Google Classroom
→ Infographic through Canva
→ Image through Adobe Spark
→ Paper Slide Video
→ Timeline using Sutori

Reflect
→ Padlet
→ Kahoot
→ Quizizz
→ Quizlet Live
→ Quizalize
→ Google Forms

Share
→ Padlet
→ Google Classroom
→ YouTube
→ Google Site
→ Social Media

Extend
→ Google Smarty Pins
→ Bonus Missions
→ Google Earth
→ Google Maps
→ Educational games related to your content

To say that reading *The HyperDoc Handbook* has impacted my teaching would be a vast understatement. HyperDocs have transformed the way I design and deliver lessons and units and have allowed me to move my classroom to a more student-centered learning environment while utilizing fabulous technology tools. When I design units, I do so while wearing HyperDoc lenses. You may have noticed that this book is even organized in keeping with a HyperDoc. I highly recommend reading *The HyperDoc Handbook!*

Try This Tomorrow

Search for HyperDocs that teachers have created before creating your own. Get a feel for what HyperDocs are and how they can help you create a more student-centered learning environment by accessing hyperdocs.co/teachers_give_teachers. Share how you use HyperDocs to enhance the learning environment of your classroom on Twitter!

#ILLUMINATEED

Learn more about designing lessons with technology at usingeducationaltechnology.com/design.

Note

Lisa Highfill, Kelly Hilston, Sara Landis, *The HyperDoc Handbook* (EdTechTeam Press: Irvine, CA, 2016).

Notes on Designing Lessons with Tech

Chapter 10
Connecting and Reflecting for Teachers

Are you using social media to enhance your teaching? How?

The availability of technology is transforming education. We are living and teaching in an amazing, pivotal time, and I could not be more excited about it! I also know that sometimes the sheer amount of technology tools can feel overwhelming. We already have so many responsibilities in our classroom, and sometimes the thought of locating a tool to use in our classroom to transform and elevate our lesson is downright scary.

It doesn't need to be this way!

Through my blog, I've found my voice as a teacher. My blog has helped me reflect upon my classroom policies and practices as well as my experiences with lessons, strategies, and tools. My blog has helped hold me accountable to constantly striving to improve my instruction and working to enhance the learning environment of my students. When we create something, whether it be a blog, a video, or an image to share with the world, we want it to be awesome. I want the information I share to be a reflection of new strategies, ideas, tools, and experiences from my classroom. I always want to be better for my students, and blogging helps push me to try new things in my classroom and share these ideas with others.

CONNECTING THROUGH BLOGGING

I started blogging in January of 2014, when I learned my school would soon be adopting a 1:1 technology initiative. Like many teachers in this position, I was intimidated by the thought of each of my students having a device. How would these devices impact student learning in my classroom? How would having these devices in my classroom change the way I taught?

Instead of going into panic mode about the upcoming classroom transition, I created a blog to serve four main purposes:

1. I wanted to curate and collect information I could use in this new learning environment.
2. I wanted to reflect upon my experiences as I implemented these new tools and strategies in my classroom.
3. I wanted to share these thoughts and experiences with other educators.
4. I wanted to interact with other educators around the world and learn from their experiences.

After writing my first blog post, I probably stared at my computer for thirty minutes before clicking the "publish" button. Questions rattled around inside my head: *Do you really have anything important to share? Is anyone going to want to read what you have to say?* If these questions are obstacles standing between you and sharing your classroom experiences through a blog, let me assuage your fears. *Yes*, you do have something important to share. Your teaching experience can provide valuable insight to other teachers. Share your experience. *Yes*, teachers all over the world are searching for strategies, lessons, tools, and ideas to use in their classroom. Don't be selfish by hoarding your classroom experiences! Reflect and share with the world. Start a blog!

CONNECTING AND REFLECTING THROUGH PROFESSIONAL LEARNING NETWORKS

Creating a professional learning network (PLN) will transform your teaching career—plain and simple. Teaching can be an isolating profession; developing a professional learning community can help you create fantastic contacts around the world. My PLN has encouraged and challenged me to design more engaging learning activities for my students. My PLN has introduced me to HyperDocs, Global Collaboration, Breakout EDU, flipped learning, and other concepts that have helped me transform my classroom.

USING TWITTER FOR REFLECTING AND CONNECTING

January 2014 was a transformational month for me as a teacher. I decided to branch out and learn as much as I could about implementing instructional technology tools to enhance the learning environment for my students. In addition to launching my blog that month, I joined Twitter. Of course, I knew about Twitter before then; the platform was becoming popular toward the end of my undergraduate studies. By the time I began teaching in 2008, it was a powerful force in the world of social media. But I didn't think it was

Think of Twitter as a stairway to an amazing water slide that will lead you to a pool of knowledge, strategies, people, and tools that you can use to make your classroom awesome.

#ILLUMINATEED

for me. After seeing how my younger sister used Twitter, I wrote it off as a fluffy, less than user-friendly social media platform that I really didn't need. I maintained that position for years even though I thoroughly enjoyed Facebook and, later, Pinterest. I just didn't see the need to join Twitter to share selfies and pictures of what I was eating for breakfast.

I am incredibly sad that I allowed that preconceived notion of Twitter and its limits to deter me from jumping onto the Twitter bandwagon sooner! Thankfully I learned about Twitter's potential for professional development at a conference. After hearing how other educators were connecting with and learning from one another, I decided it just *might* be beneficial to my teaching career. Using Twitter for professional development has not just benefitted my teaching career, it has *transformed* it! I have made so many wonderful connections with educators all over the world. I have designed lessons in collaboration with teachers from other countries via Twitter. I have created motivational programs for my students through Twitter. I have joined chats that forced me to think deeply about how I was using technology in my classroom to best meet the needs of my students. I have learned from teachers, administrators, educational technology specialists, instructional coaches, and consultants who have challenged my understanding of homework, lecture, grading, and building strong relationships with students. Think of Twitter as a stairway to an amazing water slide that will lead you to a pool of knowledge, strategies, people, and tools you can use to make your classroom awesome.

CONNECTING AND REFLECTING THROUGH OTHER SOCIAL MEDIA PLATFORMS

While Twitter is now my go-to social media account for learning, exploring, and connecting, other social media platforms, including Facebook, Pinterest, and Google+, are excellent tools for building and accessing your professional learning network! After learning about Breakout EDU and HyperDocs, I searched for and found fantastic and extremely active Facebook groups and Google+ communities about each of these topics. When I created my first digital Breakout EDU, I wanted to test it before sharing it with my students. While my husband was able to complete the activity, he wasn't able to provide me with feedback like a classroom teacher, because he's not a classroom teacher. I shared my breakout puzzle with the Facebook group, and the feedback was fantastic! Teachers commented on the post and sent me Facebook messages with questions, suggestions, or broken links. I was able to fix all the bugs and clean up any potentially confusing directions before sharing it with my students.

Pinterest, of course, is another fabulous social media platform where teachers can look for ideas, strategies, and tools to use in their classrooms. Everything from classroom decor to management strategies to content and age-specific information is available on Pinterest. Pinterest isn't just for recipes and crafts!

As teachers in the twenty-first century, we're no longer restricted to our school or district for professional development. We can interact with teachers around the world and share ideas, tools, and strategies, and forge great connections and friendships with others who are "in the trenches" with us. Using these connections, we can encourage each other to flip on the light switch in our classrooms by using educational technology tools. Jump on social media and join the conversation!

Try This Tomorrow

Create a Twitter account. This may be the best professional development you can get! Get started by searching #edchat to follow educators and engage in conversations.

#ILLUMINATEED

Learn more about how you can use technology to connect and reflect at usingeducationaltechnology.com/connecting-and-reflecting.

Notes on Connecting and
Reflecting as a Teacher with Tech

Closing Thoughts

Hopefully this book has provided you with many different ideas for using instructional technology tools to enhance your classroom learning environment. I hope you have been encouraged to use instructional technology tools to increase student engagement, all the while remembering that technology tools do not replace great teachers. You can use technology as a tool to design amazing learning experiences for your students and encourage them to collaborate, create, communicate, and think critically about their content and the world around them.

A FEW POINTS TO REMEMBER

- Don't feel like you must "do all the things" when it comes to technology integration. This causes undue stress on you as the teacher and runs the risk of creating a classroom culture not of learning but of using a tool or site that the teacher found.

- Remember to select tools that 1) enhance your lesson and 2) are easy to use.

- Pedagogy first, technology integration second.

Much like how light bulbs and the electricity that powers them enhance our lives, technology tools can enhance the learning environment for our students. Just as we use light bulbs to illuminate our homes without allowing them to become the focus of our lives, technology tools should not become the focus of your classroom. Remember, it's not about the tech; it's how you use it!

Tech Tool Index

1. **Edpuzzle** (Edpuzzle.com)

   Edpuzzle is a free tool that allows teachers to create video lessons from a variety of video sources. Teachers create a free account with Edpuzzle and can add their students through a code or by Google Classroom. Teachers can embed formative assessment activities throughout Edpuzzle video lessons as well as monitor student progress and provide fast and effective feedback.

2. **Flipgrid** (flipgrid.com)

   Flipgrid is a free tool that allows teachers to encourage student reflection and communication through video. Teachers create grids (multiple, depending on the account type) and include topics within those grids to which students should respond. Teachers can provide quick and effective feedback for their students through Flipgrid and can share the grid and topic through social media, URL, or Google Classroom.

3. **Nearpod** (nearpod.com)

   Nearpod is a free tool (with premium options) that allows teachers and students to create interactive presentations using Google Slides presentations, Microsoft PowerPoint presentations, PDF files, or lessons created through Nearpod. Teachers can embed videos, web resources, virtual fieldtrips, 3D images, and formative assessment activities into Nearpod lessons and can share those lessons with their students. Students join Nearpod lessons on any device through a code and can view and interact with the presentation on their own device. Teachers can present their lesson with or without a whiteboard and can use smartphones, tablets, or laptops to advance the presentation even if these devices are not on the same Wi-Fi network.

4. **Google Hangout** (hangouts.google.com)

   Teachers and students can use Google Hangout video calls to communicate with experts in a field, authors, or classrooms around the world!

5. **Google Classroom** (classroom.google.com)

   Google Classroom allows teachers to assign and collect evidence of student learning and provide effective feedback on student work. Teachers can distribute any type of Google Drive file through Classroom, and can also ask questions, share resources, email students, and MORE! Google Classroom has been a game changer in the classroom!

6. **BookSnaps** (tarammartin.com/BookSnaps-snapping-for-learning)

   BookSnaps, a concept developed by Tara Martin, is a fantastic way to blend technology into active reading. Using Snapchat, Google Drawings, or an augmented reality app like Gabsee, students snap a picture of an important piece of a reading and annotate the image with their thoughts through text, digital sticker, video, or Bitmoji!

7. **Google Drawing** (docs.google.com/drawings)

   An underused tool in the suite of Google tools, students can use Google Drawing to create memes, diagrams, badges, BookSnaps, and so much more!

8. **Snapchat** (snapchat.com)

   Used as part of a BookSnaps activity, for example, students can create great anecdotes for active reading strategies to share with their teacher and peers. Instead of using Snapchat to share these creations, teachers can create a Dropbox with Google Classroom or Google Forms where students submit their work.

9. **Padlet** (padlet.com)

   Using Padlet, teachers can create an interactive collaborative space for their students to brainstorm, share ideas, introduce themselves, or present information. I love to use Padlet with my students as a backchannel during class discussions or instructional videos.

10. **Answer Garden** (answergarden.ch)

    Teachers can use Answer Garden to poll their students about any topic. Student responses are populated in a word cloud that can be viewed by the class. The teacher can modify multiple settings to "turn off" the activity, require students to submit only one reply, or moderate responses.

11. **Google Sites** (sites.google.com/new)

    Using the updated version of Google Sites, teachers and students can create and share virtually anything with the world! Teachers can also modify privacy settings to only allow specific individuals or domains to access the site.

12. **IMG Flip** (imgflip.com)

    IMG Flip is one of many fantastic websites that students and teachers can use to create and share memes. Teachers can create memes to share class procedures or expectations in a fun way! Students can create memes to demonstrate their understanding of a course concept.

13. **Google Forms** (docs.google.com/forms) and **Google Sheets** (docs.google.com/spreadsheets)

    Teachers can use Google Forms in a variety of ways in the classroom; for example, teachers can create Google Forms for formative assessment and can link the form data to a Google Sheet. Teachers can then view those data in one document and can use tools like conditional formatting to visualize student learning.

14. **Google Docs** (docs.google.com)

    Students and teachers alike can benefit from the amazing Google Docs. Used in conjunction with other Google tools, Google Docs can encourage students to collaborate and communicate using technology.

15. **Google Slides** (slides.google.com)

    Google Slides also allows students and teachers to collaborate and communicate using technology. Google Slides can be used to create great, informative presentations, but also to create images, eBooks, posters, memes, and MORE!

16. **Kahoot!** (kahoot.com)

    Kahoot! is a fantastic, fun, and FREE game-based, formative assessment tool that teachers can use to gather evidence of student learning. Kahoot! provides a competitive and engaging environment for students to share what they've learned.

17. **Quizlet Live** (quizlet.com/live)

    Like Kahoot!, Quizlet Live provides a game-based learning environment for students. Teachers can launch Quizlet Live from any Quizlet flashcard deck. Students are randomly sorted into teams and must answer eleven questions in a row correctly before winning the game.

18. **Quizizz** (quizizz.com)

    Like Kahoot! and Quizlet Live, Quizizz provides a game-based learning platform. Quizizz stands out from the crowd, however, in that students view questions and response options on their individual screens and are shown memes after they respond to a question. Fun!

19. **Google Earth** (google.com/earth)

    Google Earth allows teachers to transport their students virtually anywhere in the world! Visit the Great Pyramids, the White House, and the Palace of Versailles without leaving your classroom! With new updates, Google Earth is now compatible with Google Chrome, making it the perfect solution for many classrooms.

20. **Google Arts and Culture** (google.com/culturalinstitute/beta)
    This is a great collection of information about historical events and figures, artwork, experiments, and more! Google Arts and Culture is a wonderful resource for teachers and students alike!

21. **Bitmoji** (bitmoji.com)
    Bitmoji is just fantastic. Teachers and students alike can create fun avatars to use anywhere! Bitmoji has a wonderful Chrome extension that allows users to copy and paste their Bitmoji into any creation!

22. **Ditty** (ditty.it)
    Ditty is a fun tool that teachers and students can use to put messages to music. Ditty offers free and paid songs, is easy to use, and is available for iOS and Android devices.

23. **Pandora** (pandora.com)
    Play a variety of music for your students in your classroom. Our classroom favorites are "Aerosmith on the Airwaves" or "Bach in the Bachground."

24. **Bit.ly** (bitly.com)
    Use this URL shortener to create a customized, shortened URL for any website. Bit.ly also allows users to monitor traffic to their link.

25. **Quick QR Code Generator** (bit.ly/extensionqr)
    The Quick QR Code Generator extension is one of my most-used Chrome extensions because it allows me to create a QR Code that leads to any web resource without leaving my tab!

26. **Wizer.me** (wizer.me)
    Wizer.me is a fantastic tool that teachers can use to create interactive and multi-faceted activities for their students. Teachers can embed videos, presentations, links to outside sources, and more with this great tool!

27. **Gabsee** (gabsee.com)

User Gabsee to create and share awesome augmented reality messages with your students! Teachers can design an avatar and create videos that include their avatars!

28. **QR Stuff** (qrstuff.com)

Another fantastic QR Code creator that allows users to customize the color and shape of their code as well as design QR Codes for a variety of products.

29. **TES Teach** (tes.com)

A fantastic website for teachers to locate and create lessons about anything! Teachers can create boards with a variety of curated content for their students. Students can access the lesson through link, Google Classroom, social media, or QR Code.

30. **Quizalize** (quizalize.com)

Another great game-based formative assessment tool. Quizalize allows teachers to sync their Google Classroom roster with the game, which can make monitoring student progress easier!

31. **Adobe Spark** (spark.adobe.com)

A free and easy-to-use image and video creation site.

32. **Remind** (remind.com)

A fantastic platform that teachers can use to communicate and share information with students and parents. All Remind conversations are saved and can be accessed by school administration.

33. **Sutori** (sutori.com)

Formerly known as HSTRY, Sutori offers teachers and students the ability to create interactive timelines. These timelines can include images, videos, quizzes, and more!

34. **Google Street View** (google.com/streetview)

Students and teachers can create and share their own virtual reality images with Google Street view! For *free*!

35. **Flippity** (flippity.net)

Students and teachers can use Flippity to create flash cards, game-show style review activities, BINGO games, and much more. Flippity requires the use of a Google Spreadsheet to create these activities, which means all the activities can be accessed via Google Drive.

Acknowledgments

I am beyond grateful for the opportunity to share these tools and ideas with you in this book! Throughout the process of writing *Illuminate*, I kept many inspirational phrases and verses posted around my workspace, but the most influential was from Psalm 46:5, "God is within her, she will not fall." This verse has continued to motivate, encourage, and comfort me!

I am incredibly thankful to my husband, Issac, for his continuous love and support of me and my ambitious plans. My daughters, Hanna and Molly, have been the biggest blessings I could have ever hoped for in my life and have pushed me, without their knowledge, to continue to aspire to be the best version of myself and to be someone they can be proud to say is their Mommy. Throughout my entire life, my parents have motivated and encouraged me to always "do your best" in all avenues of life, and simply thanking them with words will never be enough to show the love and gratitude I have for them. My sister, Brittany, has encouraged me to be a person whom she can look up to and be proud to call her sister.

I've also been so fortunate to work in a district and building with administrators who are incredibly supportive and who have encouraged me to take risks with my instructional strategies with the best interest of my students in mind. I've been blessed with fantastic students throughout my teaching career who have inspired me to seek out strategies that I can employ to create a more engaging and dynamic learning environment for them.

I am blessed with the support of Dave Burgess Consulting, Inc., who listened to my idea to share strategies, tools, and reflections to help teachers use instructional technology to enhance the learning environment and increase student engagement!

Thank you for reading *Illuminate*! You rock! Please follow my blog, *Teaching with Technology* (usingeducationaltechnology.com) to keep up with reflections, strategies, tips, and tools from my flipped, blended, and gamified classroom!

MORE FROM

DAVE BURGESS
Consulting, Inc.

Since 2012, DBCI has been publishing books that inspire and equip educators to be their best. For more information on our DBCI titles or to purchase bulk orders for your school, district, or book study, visit **DaveBurgessconsulting.com/DBCIbooks**.

More from the *Like a PIRATE™* Series

Teach Like a PIRATE by Dave Burgess

eXPlore Like a Pirate by Michael Matera

Learn Like a Pirate by Paul Solarz

Play Like a Pirate by Quinn Rollins

Run Like a Pirate by Adam Welcome

Lead Like a PIRATE™ Series

Lead Like a PIRATE by Shelley Burgess and Beth Houf

Balance Like a Pirate by Jessica Cabeen, Jessica Johnson, and Sarah Johnson

Lead beyond Your Title by Nili Bartley

Lead with Culture by Jay Billy

Lead with Literacy by Mandy Ellis

Leadership & School Culture

Culturize by Jimmy Casas

Escaping the School Leader's Dunk Tank by Rebecca Coda and Rick Jetter

From Teacher to Leader by Starr Sackstein

The Innovator's Mindset by George Couros

Kids Deserve It! by Todd Nesloney and Adam Welcome

Let Them Speak by Rebecca Coda and Rick Jetter

The Limitless School by Abe Hege and Adam Dovico

The Pepper Effect by Sean Gaillard

The Principled Principal by Jeffrey Zoul and Anthony McConnell

Relentless by Hamish Brewer

The Secret Solution by Todd Whitaker, Sam Miller, and Ryan Donlan

Start. Right. Now. by Todd Whitaker, Jeffrey Zoul, and Jimmy Casas

Stop. Right. Now. by Jimmy Casas and Jeffrey Zoul

They Call Me "Mr. De" by Frank DeAngelis

Unmapped Potential by Julie Hasson and Missy Lennard

Word Shift by Joy Kirr

Your School Rocks by Ryan McLane and Eric Lowe

Technology & Tools

50 Things You Can Do with Google Classroom by Alice Keeler and Libbi Miller

50 Things to Go Further with Google Classroom by Alice Keeler and Libbi Miller

140 Twitter Tips for Educators by Brad Currie, Billy Krakower, and Scott Rocco

Block Breaker by Brian Aspinall

Code Breaker by Brian Aspinall

Google Apps for Littles by Christine Pinto and Alice Keeler

Master the Media by Julie Smith

Shake Up Learning by Kasey Bell

Social LEADia by Jennifer Casa-Todd

Teaching Math with Google Apps by Alice Keeler and Diana Herrington

Teachingland by Amanda Fox and Mary Ellen Weeks

Teaching Methods & Materials

All 4s and 5s by Andrew Sharos

Boredom Busters by Katie Powell

The Classroom Chef by John Stevens and Matt Vaudrey

Ditch That Homework by Matt Miller and Alice Keeler

Ditch That Textbook by Matt Miller

Don't Ditch That Tech by Matt Miller, Nate Ridgway, and
  Angelia Ridgway

EDrenaline Rush by John Meehan

Educated by Design by Michael Cohen, The Tech Rabbi

The EduProtocol Field Guide by Marlena Hebern and Jon Corippo

The EduProtocol Field Guide: Book 2 by Marlena Hebern and
  Jon Corippo

Instant Relevance by Denis Sheeran

LAUNCH by John Spencer and A.J. Juliani

Make Learning MAGICAL by Tisha Richmond

Pure Genius by Don Wettrick

The Revolution by Darren Ellwein and Derek McCoy

Shift This! by Joy Kirr

Spark Learning by Ramsey Musallam

Sparks in the Dark by Travis Crowder and Todd Nesloney

Table Talk Math by John Stevens

The Wild Card by Hope and Wade King

The Writing on the Classroom Wall by Steve Wyborney

Inspiration, Professional Growth & Personal Development

Be REAL by Tara Martin

Be the One for Kids by Ryan Sheehy

Creatively Productive by Lisa Johnson

Educational Eye Exam by Alicia Ray

The EduNinja Mindset by Jennifer Burdis

Empower Our Girls by Lynmara Colón and Adam Welcome

The Four O'Clock Faculty by Rich Czyz

How Much Water Do We Have? by Pete and Kris Nunweiler

P Is for Pirate by Dave and Shelley Burgess

A Passion for Kindness by Tamara Letter

The Path to Serendipity by Allyson Apsey

Sanctuaries by Dan Tricarico

The SECRET SAUCE by Rich Czyz

Shattering the Perfect Teacher Myth by Aaron Hogan

Stories from Webb by Todd Nesloney

Talk to Me by Kim Bearden

Teach Me, Teacher by Jacob Chastain

Through the Lens of Serendipity by Allyson Apsey

The Zen Teacher by Dan Tricarico

Children's Books

Beyond Us by Aaron Polansky

Dolphins in Trees by Aaron Polansky

I Want to Be a Lot by Ashley Savage

The Princes of Serendip by Allyson Apsey

Zom-Be a Design Thinker by Amanda Fox

ABOUT THE AUTHOR

Bethany Petty is a Christian, mother, wife, full-time high school social studies teacher, adjunct instructor of educational technology, reader, runner, blogger, and coffee junkie. Bethany regularly blogs at *Teaching with Technology*, where she shares resources, ideas, EdTech tools, and tips and tricks as well as reflections from her blended/flipped/gamified high school social studies classroom. Bethany's blog was recently listed as one of *EdTech Magazine's* 50 K–12 IT Blogs to Read. She was named a finalist in *EdTech Digest's* 2017 Awards in the School Leader category and was listed as one of the top one hundred Flipped Learning teachers worldwide (2017). Bethany was a Spotlight Educator at the 2018 METC conference and was recently  awarded the 2018 VFW National Citizenship Teacher of the Year Award for VFW Post #5741 and for VFW District 8 in Missouri. She has published posts on Edutopia, Fractus Learning, Sophia Learning, and Whooo's Reading and has presented at multiple technology conferences.

Bethany graduated from Southeast Missouri State University in 2008 with her BSEd in secondary education with a social studies concentration. She graduated from the University of Missouri-Columbia in 2011 with her masters' degree in teaching and learning. She has earned additional hours in History from Missouri State University.

Bethany is a Google Certified Teacher, Google Certified Trainer, Apple Teacher, Nearpod PioNear, Edpuzzle Pioneer, Remind Connected Educator, and a Flipped Learning Global Ambassador. Bethany conducts professional development sessions in her school district and the surrounding area.

Bethany, her husband, Issac, and their daughters, Hanna and Molly, live in Missouri.